Children's Sermons
A to Z

Brett Blair
and
Tim Carpenter

CSS Publishing Company, Inc., Lima, Ohio

FIRST EDITION
Copyright © 2000 by
Brett Blair

This book is available in the following formats, listed by ISBN:
0-7880-1780-2   Book
0-7880-1781-0   Disk
0-7880-1782-9   Sermon Prep

PRINTED IN U.S.A.

To Hannah Blair
and
To Jordan and Ethan Carpenter

Table Of Contents

EPIPHANY

EASTER

PENTECOST

Foreword

I am convinced that the Children's Sermon has only begun to find its way into the mainstream. For thirty years this moment in the worship service has primarily been the focus of mainline churches, but lately other traditions of Christianity are discovering the value of this time in which true spontaneity takes place and anything can happen.

These children's sermons predominantly use props to illustrate their points. In addition to props, Reverend Tim Carpenter and I have used an additional technique throughout. The sermons are broken up into two main parts: the lesson and the application. The lesson attempts to engage the children, through the use of the prop, in teaching the teacher. This method makes the children active rather than passive participants. Each lesson's conclusion contains an "ah-ha" moment which becomes the transition or the bridge for the application of the scripture.

While the book is laid out following the Revised Common Lectionary, you may also look sermons up by scripture using the index in the back. Two messages have been written for each Sunday: one from the Gospels (Brett Blair) and one from the Epistles (Tim Carpenter).

The following method is used to guide the teacher: bold type instructs how to carry out the sermon. Regular print suggests the words which are to be spoken by the teacher. Italicized words in parentheses contain the responses of the children.

Anyone who has done children's sermons for any length of time has heard the following words from the adults, "I learn more from the children's sermon than I do from the real sermon." By "real" they mean "adult," but there is a lesson here for all those who attempt to preach or teach. The truths of scripture are so simple that even a child can understand them.

Grace and Peace,
Reverend Brett Blair

ADVENT

Advent 1
Luke 21:25-36

Expect The Unexpected

Exegetical Aim: When Jesus comes back it will be a surprise.

Props: A clock will be needed for the opening. In addition to the clock you may use one of the following to interrupt the silent period mentioned below: 1) A fog horn. 2) A horn instrument of some kind. 3) Someone who has been away from the church — on vacation — and has returned. They will burst into the sanctuary with a suitcase saying, "I'm back." They will then sit down with the children and discuss their travels and their return home. 4) Use no other props — only the clock — and after the silent period is over discuss their expectations.

Lesson: Good morning. What is this? *(clock)* What does a clock tell us? *(what time it is)* That's right. It tells us the time of day. I have another question. Can a clock tell us what's going to happen? *(no)* Why not? *(response)* What time is it right now? *(response)* The small hand is on the 11 and the big hand is on the 20. That means it's 11:20. Okay. That's the time. Now, I wonder what is going to happen right now. What do you think is going to happen? *(response)* Let's wait and see. **Wait in silence 10-15 seconds. Look around as if something might happen.** Did anything happen? *(response)* Let's wait just a little bit more. **Look around again. After 10-15 seconds the unexpected event should take place. Example: Have someone sound the horn from the choir.**
What happened? *(response)* Did you know that was going to happen? *(response)*

Application: Sometimes things happen unexpectedly. The Bible tells us that we need to expect the unexpected, to be ready at all

15

times because one day Jesus will return to this world. So when you least expect it **pause and look around** Jesus will return to earth and we will be with him. **Looking back at the clock:** It might be today, right now at 11:25 in the morning, or it might be tomorrow. Let's keep watching.

Let's Pray: Dear Lord, we do not know when you will return and it may surprise us but we will keep watch and we will be ready. Amen.

Advent 1
1 Thessalonians 3:9-13

Erasing Blame

Exegetical Aim: To demonstrate that Christ's love makes us blameless.

Props: A chalkboard, some chalk, and an eraser.

Lesson: When I was a little boy, I went to school. And in the school we had a chalkboard where we would do all of our work in front of the class. Do any of you have chalkboards in your classroom? *(response)* Sometimes we would do math problems. The teacher would write a math problem for us on the board and we would have to solve it. Let me show you. **Write 2+2= on the board and ask someone to write the answer with the chalk. Then quickly do another simple problem and allow someone else to write the answer.** The thing I remember most about that chalkboard, though, is that it wasn't always used for doing problems. Do you know what else it was used for? *(response)* Whenever the teacher had to leave the room, she would appoint one of the children in the class to take names of anyone who was talking while she was gone. Does your teacher ever do that? *(response)* I remember that it was an awful feeling to have one's name put on the board. Because if the teacher saw that name, what would happen? *(response)* Yes, you would get in trouble. Sometimes we would do different things to try to persuade the monitor to take our name off of the board. Sometimes we would bribe them with bubble gum, or promise them other things, and they would erase our name. And that was always a good feeling. If your name is not on the board, you won't get in trouble.

Application: In 1 Thessalonians 3:13, the Apostle Paul said something about not having any blame. He said that Christ makes our hearts "blameless" before God. Say that with me. "Christ makes ... our hearts ... blameless ... before God." In other words, all of us

17

have messed up before, right? *(response)* We have taken a toy that wasn't ours, or we didn't mind our mom or dad, or we called someone a name. I have messed up before, too. **Write your own name on the board.** But the good news is that when we love Jesus, we can call out to him and he will ... do what? *(response)* That's right. **Erase your name.** He will erase our names from the chalkboard. He will erase our guilt. And when God looks at the board of blame, will he see your name up there? No. He will see you as the holy person you are intended to be! So the next time you see a chalkboard, just remember the verse, and say it with me again, "Christ makes ... our hearts ... blameless ... before God."

Let's Pray: Thank you, God, that you sent Christ into the world. Thank you that in his name and through his love we are made "blameless." In Jesus' name. Amen.

Advent 2
Luke 3:1-6

The Shortest Distance Between Two Points

Exegetical Aim: We should allow God direct access to our lives. Key verse: 5b.

Props: Large map of your city, state, or country, and two large washable markers of different colors. One should be red. The red should easily overpower the other color. Unfold the map and place it on the ground before the children arrive. Have them sit around it. Make sure the markers are not permanent.

Lesson: Good morning! *(response)* I want everyone to sit around our piece of paper. What is this? *(a map)* Does anyone know what it is a map of? *(response)* That's right it is a map of the city. Can any of you find your home? **Allow time for them to search.** What about the church? Can anyone find the church? **Allow them to search.** I am going to help you find the church. The church is right here. What are all these lines on the map? *(streets)* **Show them the streets that surround the church and a couple of landmarks in the neighborhood.**

There is one more thing I want you to try to find. Can anyone find the zoo? *(response)* **You could also pick three or four landmarks on the four corners of the map from which various teams can start. The museum, the park, and the McDonald's are other possibilities. This is not a race. You are letting them carefully and exactly trace the paths between the church and the landmarks.**

I want you to take this marker and follow the streets drawing a path from the zoo to the church. **A majority of time may be spent here. When they are done:** Show me how to get to the zoo. It really took a lot of twists and turns to get to the zoo. How many turns did you have to make? *(response)* The roads are really crooked, aren't they? *(response)* I have a question for you. If you were going to build a quick road between the zoo and the church, how would you build that road? *(straight)* Here is a red marker. Show me what that road would look like. **A ruler or yard stick to aid in the drawing of the line would help here.**

Application: When they are done, hold up the map for everyone to see. Now you can see all the crooked roads and turns we have to take. **Have a child show the congregation the crooked path by tracing the path with his/her finger.** But if we could, we would make straight roads. **Have another child show the straight path.** Isaiah, in the Bible, talked about making the crooked roads straight and making the rough ways smooth. He was telling us to get ready for God and to give him a straight road into our lives. We shouldn't make God take a left turn and then a right turn and give him crooked roads to travel. God wants us to open our hearts and let him in right now.

Let's Pray: God, we are going to make straight paths for you to come into our lives. We open our hearts fully to your Son, Jesus Christ. Amen.

Advent 2
Philippians 1:3-11

Abounding Love

Exegetical Aim: To demonstrate that God's desire is for our love to abound more and more.

Props: A pitcher of water, a large glass, and a pan.

Lesson: Good morning. Look at what I have today. **Hold up the pitcher of water.** I thought that today I might get thirsty, so I brought some water just in case. I think I'm kind of thirsty now, as a matter of fact. Do you mind if I have a drink? *(response)* Thank you. **Bring out the large glass.** Do you think that this is big enough to quench my thirst? *(response)* Good. Well, there's one more thing I had better do before I pour the water. I'm afraid that I might mess up while I am pouring the water. What might happen? *(response)* Yes, I might spill it. So I'm going to place this pan underneath the glass just in case I spill some. How about that? Here we go. **Pour the water slowly into the glass until it is three-quarters of the way full.** Do you think that's enough? Maybe I should fill it all the way? *(response)* Okay, let's fill it all the way. **Carefully fill it to the rim without spilling any.** There we go. It's full now. Do you think that it can get any fuller? *(response)* What would happen if I were to pour more water into the cup? *(response)* **Look at the children and begin to pour the water into the glass. Let the water spill out over the edge of the glass into the pan. While you are pouring continue to ask the children what would happen if you poured more water into the cup. This should create some laughing and some squeals.** Oops. What happened? *(response)* Yes, it appears that I poured more water than the glass would hold. But wait a minute. Didn't you tell me to fill the glass? *(response)* Isn't it still full? *(response)* Even though the water spilled out of the glass, the glass is still full.

Application: That's the way it is with love. You can never be too full of love. Once you are full of love, what happens to all of the other love inside of you? *(response)* Yes! It pours out all over the place. Have you ever known someone who was always pouring out love to other people? *(response)* You know, Jesus was like that, too. When someone is always pouring out love, we say that that person is "abounding" in love. And to be abounding in love, you have to be full of love, don't you? Well, the Apostle Paul told the people in the early church that he wanted them to have a lot of love. He said, "It is my prayer that your love will abound more and more." How can we be filled with love? *(response)* By letting Jesus fill our hearts. So the next time you see a glass of water, remember that just as water that overflows from a glass still leaves the glass full, love flowing out of us leaves us full of love.

Let's Pray: Lord, fill us up with your love. Amen.

How Should We Live?

Exegetical Aim: To convey John the Baptist's understanding of compassion.

Props: Two heavy coats. One worn on top of the other.

Lesson: G-G-Good m-m-morning! It's freezing out here. Aren't you cold? *(response)* You're not? My fingers are frozen. **Blow your breath into your hands to warm them. Call one of the children up to sit beside you. You will be getting him or her to participate.** Josh, come up here and sit beside me and maybe we can stay warm together. **When the child arrives, sit there a moment acting cold. In a loud whisper so others can hear:** You're supposed to act cold, Okay? *(okay)* **Normal voice:** J-J-Josh, isn't it c-c-cold out here? *(yes)* **In a loud whisper:** No, you're supposed to say, "y-y-yes." Okay? *(okay)* J-J-Josh, isn't it c-c-cold out here? *(y-y-yes)* **If the child is not hugging himself and shaking, place his arms in that position.**

You look c-c-cold. I'm feeling pretty warm though in my nice TWO big coats. Don't you like my coats, Josh? *(response)* I can't imagine being out on a night like this without a coat, can you? *(response)* **Address the rest of the children:** Can you imagine someone being out in the cold without a coat? *(response)* What's wrong? *(response)* Who doesn't have a coat? *(Josh)* Yeah, you're right, he doesn't. He must be cold! Are you cold? *(y-y-yes)* Yep, you're right. He's c-c-cold. **Rub your hands together and look around casually.** Maybe it will get warmer tomorrow.

Application: Is there something wrong? *(response)* I should give him one of my coats? Why? *(response)* Oh, would you like one of my coats? *(response)* I really don't need two coats. **Put the coat on him.** Are you warm now? *(response)* I wasn't being very nice, was I? *(response)* This is how we are supposed to live as Christians. There's a fellow in the Bible by the name of John the Baptist, and someone asked him, "How should we live our lives?" John told him, "The man who has two coats should share with him who has none, and the one who has food should share with him who has none." Let's share the things that we have with one another.

Let's Pray: Lord, we want to share our coats, our food, and our toys with those who have none. Teach us to love one another. Amen.

Advent 3
Philippians 4:4-7

At Hand

Exegetical Aim: To demonstrate the nearness of God.

Props: None needed.

Lesson: Good morning. Today I want you to help me with a game. The game is called "Near and Far." Would you like me to show you how it works? *(response)* Okay. Here goes. I will call out the name of something that is in this church, and I want you to tell me if it is near or far. **Call out three things in the sanctuary that are far away and three things that are near enough to be reached by your hand. Have the children call out "far" or "near" depending on each thing.** How did you know what was near to me? *(response)* Did you notice that I can reach out and touch with my hand everything that was near? **Demonstrate by quickly reaching out and touching the things that were called out as near.** These things are near because they are close to my hand. We have a phrase that means "near." The phrase is, "At hand," because things that are near are at our hands.

Application: The Apostle Paul wanted us to remember that about Jesus Christ. He said that we should always be living for Christ because the Lord is at hand. So we don't have to worry when things look bad, because even when things go wrong, who is at hand? *(Jesus)* Yes. The Lord is at hand. So the next time you look at your hand, remember to say thank you to God for letting Jesus Christ be so near to us. Remember the Bible verse. Say it with me: The Lord is at hand.

Let's Pray: Thank you, God, for Jesus Christ. Thank you that the Lord is at hand, that he is always near. Amen.

Advent 4
Luke 1:39-45

What Can God Do?

Exegetical Aim: God can do some awesome things.

Props: A Bible and photographs (or replicas) of some big things: elephant, tree, world, stars, or universe. The bigger the photo the better.

Lesson: Good morning. *(response)* How is everyone doing? *(response)* Here is a question for you this morning, and I think you know the answer to it. How big is God? *(response)* Tell me. **Show the respective pictures:** Is God bigger than an elephant? *(response)* **Sound incredulous:** How is he bigger than an elephant? *(response)* Is God bigger than a tree? *(response)* How is God bigger than a tree? *(response)* Is God bigger than the world? *(response)* How can God be bigger than the world? *(response)* Okay, I know this one is impossible. Is God bigger than the universe? *(response)* Now how can he be bigger than the stars and the whole universe? *(response)* But that's the biggest thing ever! How can he be bigger than the universe? *(response)* **For a touch of humor you might add as the very last question a picture of someone famous who will create laughter.**

Application: Slowly as if you are thinking this through: Okay. If God is bigger than an elephant and he is bigger than a tree, if he is even bigger than the world and the stars and the whole universe, then how can God be a baby and fit inside Mary's tummy? *(response)* **Have the appropriate text marked:** It says right here in Luke chapter 1 verse 43 that Mary was the mother of our Lord. How can that be? How can God who is bigger than all things be a baby? In Mary's tummy? *(response)*

That's the amazing thing about God. He is so big and strong and powerful that he even can become a baby in Mary's tummy. He can do whatever he chooses. He can be bigger than the world or he can be small like when he came to earth as the baby Jesus. But the most amazing thing of all is that he became a small baby because he loved us and he wanted to be with us. God is so amazing and so good.

Let's Pray: God, we know that you are greater than all the trees and stars and things that are. And even though you are so much bigger than us, you became one of us and loved us. Amen

Advent 4
Hebrews 10:5-10

The Best Present

Exegetical Aim: To demonstrate that God is pleased with
obedience.

Props: Some boxes wrapped for Christmas.

Lesson: Well! What is going to happen this week? *(response)* That's
right. Christmas is coming. And we all know what that means.
Presents! Who here is going to get presents on Christmas Day?
(response) And who will give presents this Christmas? *(response)*
What kind of gifts are good to give? *(response)* I'm going to give
some presents, too. **Hold up some of the wrapped boxes for the
children to see.** Some are big and some are small. But all of them
are to people who are special to me, and so I want to show them
how much I care about them. Isn't that why we give presents? Just
as the wise men brought gifts to Jesus, we give gifts on the birthday of Jesus to show people how much we love them.

A long time ago, people used to bring all sorts of gifts to God
to show God how much they loved him. They called these gifts
sacrifices. But Jesus came and showed us that what God really
wants is for us to give ourselves to God.

Application: I want to share with you a scripture this morning.
The scripture comes from Hebrews 10, and in it Jesus says, "Lo, I
have come to do your will." Jesus knew that the best gift he could
give to God was obedience. Jesus gave himself fully to God and
obeyed him. And so as Christians, what would be the best present
that we could give to God? *(response)* That's right, our obedience
and ourselves. It's really nice to give gifts to our loved ones. This
Christmas Day, I want you to enjoy that time, and appreciate anything that is given to you. But when you sit down next to that Christmas tree with all the presents under it, I want you to remember that
the best gift you can give to God and to your parents is to give

yourself fully in obedience. Just like Jesus said to his Father, "Lo, I have come to do your will."

Let's Pray: We thank you, God, that Jesus came into the world. Thank you for letting him show us that all you really want is for us to give you our lives. In Jesus' name. Amen.

CHRISTMAS

Christmas Day
John 1:1-18

God Became Human

Exegetical Aim: To teach the incarnation.

Props: Fingers and Toes.

Lesson: Good morning! Hey, do you know what's going to happen in a few days? *(response)* I will give you a hint: Happy New Year! Now do you know what will happen? *(response)* It will be a new year! What year will it be? *(response)* You know what that means; we're all getting a little older. How old are you now? *(response)* Let's see ... **hold up the respective amount of fingers as you ask the following** how many of you are three? Four? Five? Six? Wow, that's pretty old, isn't it. Do you know how old I am? *(response)* **Interact with the children until they guess your age.** Now that you've guessed how old I am, how old is your dad? *(response)* Is that old? *(response)* Well, here's the really important question: How old is your mom? *(response)* That's not old at all, is it? *(response)* Let me tell you a secret. When you say your mom's age you always say "29." That way you always get ice cream.

I have another question? Do you think that your dad — how old did you say he was? — do you think your dad being *so old* could be five years old again? *(response)* Do you think he could become a child? *(response)* He couldn't? Why not? *(response)* What about your mom? Do you think your mom will ever be five years old again? *(response)* Why not? *(response)* Do you think she will ever be 29 again? Don't answer that!

Application: Can you think of anyone who was really old and then became five years old? *(response)* You can't think of anyone who was old and then became a child? *(response)* Well, the Bible tells us that this really happened. In the Gospel of John, John says, "The Word became flesh and lived among us." Can anyone tell me what that means, "the Word became flesh and lived with us?" *(Jesus was born)* Yes, that's it. So it has happened. Not to your dad or your mom, but to Jesus. You see Jesus is actually millions and millions of years old — just a little older than your dad — and he lived in heaven. How many is a million? **Hold up five fingers:** This many? *(response)* **Hold up ten fingers:** This many? *(response)* **Hold up your toes and continue the questioning by having them hold up their fingers and then their toes. Observing all the toes and fingers:** Look at how many Jesus is. You see, he's older than the stars because he is God and he lived in heaven. But, then he decided to leave heaven and come to earth and live with us. So, you see, Jesus isn't just a little baby. He is God in heaven who was very old and became a baby. He became a little child and he lived as a little child. He knew what it meant to have chickenpox and get a fever. He knew what it meant to fall down and skin his knees and go to bed early. He knows what it means to be three **Hold up your fingers** and four and five and six ... and even 29. God himself who is older than the stars knows what it is like to be a little boy.

Let's Pray: Dear God, it is wonderful that you know what it is like to be five and six and seven years old. What is even more wonderful is you did it for us. Amen.

Christmas Day
Hebrews 1:1-4 (5-12)

Leaving Prints

Exegetical Aim: To demonstrate that Jesus Christ is the "exact imprint" of God's very being.

Props: An ink pad and construction paper and enough pieces of paper for each child. On each piece of paper write, "Christ is the exact imprint of God's very being" (Hebrews 1:3).

Lesson: I want to show you something really neat this morning. **Bring out the ink pad.** This is an ink pad. When I open it up, there is a pad that has ink inside of it. One neat thing we can do with an ink pad is make fingerprints. Who knows why people have their fingerprints taken? **Guide the children in discussing a couple of different reasons: i.e., the police want them if they catch a criminal, or parents want them just in case their children get lost, etc.** Do you know what is so special about a fingerprint? *(response)* A fingerprint is unique. Only one person in the whole world has your fingerprint — you. So if I take my thumb and press it on the ink pad, and then put my thumb on the paper, it will leave my print. Watch this. **Demonstrate making your thumbprint.** Today, I have special paper that I want you each to have. **Hand the paper to each child.** And in a minute I want you to put your thumbprint on the paper just like I have done.

Application: This morning is a special day. Do you know what today is? *(response)* Yes, it is Christmas Day! What is special about Christmas Day? *(response)* That is correct; it is the day that Jesus was born! Do you know who the Bible says that Jesus was? *(response)* The Bible says that Jesus is the exact imprint of God's being ... the *exact* imprint. Now, if only I can leave a fingerprint that is mine, what do you suppose it means if Jesus Christ is the exact imprint of God's being? Only who could have sent Jesus to the earth? *(response)* That's right. Only God could have sent Jesus, because Jesus is God's imprint sent to earth. This Christmas Day, I want you to remember that if you want to see God, you just need to see ... who? *(response)* That is correct. To see God, we need to look to Jesus. Because Jesus is the exact imprint of God's being.

Direct the children in making a thumbprint in the paper you have passed to them. Now I want you each to press your thumb on the pad, and then place your thumb on the paper that I gave you. On that paper is written the Bible verse that I just told you about. Whenever you look at your thumbprint, a print that only you can leave, you can remember that Jesus was the imprint that only God could leave ... on this Christmas Day!

Let's Pray: Thank you, God, for sending Jesus to be your exact imprint. Help us to remember that when we want to know what you are like, we just need to look to Jesus. In his name we pray. Amen.

Christmas 1
Luke 2:41-52

My Father's House

Exegetical Aim: The sanctity of the church.

Props: A stepstool or small stepladder in front of the pulpit and the ability to take the children around the different stations of the sanctuary.

Lesson: Good morning! *(response)* Everyone feeling well this morning? *(response)* Can anyone tell me about their father's house? *(response)* Tell me some things that are in your father's house? *(response)* This morning I want to show you around my Father's house. Everyone stand up and walk with me. **Walk up to the communion table.** Look around. This is my Father's house. Tell me what you see? *(response)* **Take some time and allow the children to name various objects. When they are named, give some explanation as to their purpose.**

Assuming no one points out the communion table: We are standing in front of a table. Can anyone tell me what this table is for? *(response)* This table is the communion table. It reminds us that Jesus died for us. We put the Bread and Wine on top of this table because they remind us that Jesus' body was broken for us and that he bled for us.

Let's go over here. What is this? *(response)* This is called the pulpit. I want everyone to stand up in the pulpit and look out at everyone. If you want to say, "Hi," you can. **As they are helped up into the pulpit:** What does the minister do here each week? *(response)* I tell everyone about our heavenly Father and how to love him and love our neighbors.

So the next time you bring a friend to church you can tell them, "This is my Father's house." This is a holy place and I love this place as much as I do my own home.

Now I am going to step up into the pulpit. **If you are using a stepstool bring some levity to the moment by stepping upon the stool.** Hi! **Offer the prayer from the pulpit.**

Let's Pray: Father, this is your house. All around me are signs of your love for me. I love to be here with all the children of God. Amen.

Christmas 1
Colossians 3:12-17

Ruling Peace

Exegetical Aim: To teach the need for Christ's peace to rule in our lives.

Props: A chess set.

Lesson: Good morning. Did you all have a nice Christmas morning? *(response)* What are some of the things that you received? *(response)*

Well, this morning, I want to talk to you about the gift of a king. Jesus is our king. And when he was born in Bethlehem, the king of the universe was born. Now when he was born, did he come with a lot of soldiers? *(response)* Did he walk around and give a lot of orders? *(response)* No. He came peacefully, didn't he? He was just a little baby.

Does anyone know what this is? **Hold up the chess board with some of the pieces on it.** *(response)* Yes. It's a chess board. And the chess board has a lot of pieces. There are pawns, and knights, and bishops, and queens, and rooks. **As you call out the names of the pieces, hold them up for the children to see.** But do you know what the most important piece in chess is? *(response)* That's right. This tall piece called the king is the most important piece. Kings are important people, aren't they? If a king tells you to do something, you have to do it. Right? *(response)* A king is ruler of his kingdom. His word is what matters most in that kingdom.

Application: Did you know that you have a kingdom right inside of you? Where do you think God makes his kingdom? *(response)* Yes, in our hearts. **Holding up the king:** Let me ask you. Who is the ruler of your kingdom? *(response)* The Apostle Paul said, "Let the peace of Christ rule in your hearts." If the peace of Christ rules our hearts, then we shouldn't be afraid and we shouldn't worry. If someone treats us badly, do we treat them badly? *(response)* No, because the peace of Christ rules our hearts. And if someone calls us a name, do we call them a name in return? *(response)* No, because the peace of Christ rules our hearts. There are times when you're going to have trouble all around you. What will you do? *(response)* Let the peace of Christ rule your heart. So in everything we do and say, remember that Jesus Christ is our king, and his peace rules. The next time you are scared, worried, troubled, or mad, remember what rules our hearts. The peace of Christ does.

Let's Pray: We thank you, God, that we celebrate Christmas. Thank you that Jesus came to bring peace, and that he is our king. Help us always to let his peace rule in our hearts. Amen.

EPIPHANY

Epiphany
Matthew 2:1-12

Who Is Jesus?

Exegetical Aim: To give an understanding of John's prologue and his understanding of Jesus' nature.

Props: Flash Cards: nine pieces of paper with the following words boldly written: WORD, GOD, LIFE, LIGHT, FLESH, GLORY, GRACE , TRUTH, ONE and ONLY. Distribute the words around the sanctuary for the children to find. You will need a good grasp of the sequence of the words and the basic development of John's thought. It is necessary to commit to memory the following synopsis of John's prologue: So Jesus is the Word who was God and in him was life. And, Jesus' life has given us light. Then the Word became flesh and lived among us. In him we see God's glory. He is full of grace and truth. And, he is the one and only. There are no others.

Lesson: Good morning. *(response)* I have always wondered, "Who is Jesus?" There is a book in the Bible that helps me understand who Jesus is. The book is by a man named John, and John tried to describe Jesus. This morning I want you to go out into the sanctuary and find some words; these are words that John used to describe Jesus. **Assign one person or two person teams to find each word or set of words as you retell John's prologue.** [Child's name], would you please go out and find the piece of paper that says WORD. John said that in the very beginning of the world, before any thing else existed, before there were stars or moons or even starfish, there was the WORD. What do you think John meant when he called Jesus the Word? *(response)* **Hold up the paper:**

- So Jesus is the Word.

Now, [Child's name], go find the word GOD. John also said that the Word was GOD. What do you think John meant when he said that Jesus was God? *(response)* **Flip the cards in sequence:**

- So Jesus is the Word who was God.

Now, [Children's names], go find the words LIFE and LIGHT. John also said that in Jesus was LIFE. What do you think John meant when he said that Life was in Jesus? *(response)* Maybe this will help you a little: He also said that this Life was our LIGHT. **Flip the cards in sequence:**

- So Jesus is the Word who was God and in him was life. And, Jesus' life has given us light.

[Child's name], go find the word FLESH. John also said that the Word became FLESH. What do you think John meant when he said that the Word became FLESH? *(response)* It's amazing but what that means is that God himself became a person, and we call him Jesus. **Flip the cards in sequence:**

- So Jesus is the Word who was God and in him was life. And, Jesus' life has given us light. Then the Word became flesh and lived among us.

[Children's names], go find the words GLORY, GRACE, and TRUTH. John also said that in Jesus we have seen God's glory — that Jesus is full of GRACE and TRUTH. What do you think John meant by that? *(response)* **Flip the cards in sequence:**

- So Jesus is the Word who was God and in him was life. And, Jesus' life has given us light. Then the Word became flesh and lived among us. In him we see God's glory. He is full of grace and truth.

[Children's names], go find the words ONE and ONLY. John said a lot of things, didn't he? Well, here is the last of them. John said

40

that Jesus is the One and Only. What do you think John meant by that? *(response)* **Flip the cards in sequence:**

- Here is what John said about Jesus: **Hold all the cards above your head and flip through them — allow the children to say each word as you come to them.** Jesus is the *(Word)* who was *(God)* and in him was *(life)*. And, Jesus' life has given us *(light)*. Then the Word became *(flesh)* and lived among us. In him we see God's *(glory)*. He is full of *(grace)* and *(truth)*. And, he is the *(One)* and *(Only)*. There are no others.

John used a lot of words to describe Jesus, and whenever I am trying to figure out who Jesus is, I turn to the beginning of John's book and read these words, and they help me understand.

Let's Pray: Father, you have sent your One and Only Son to us, and we have received life through him. Thank you for your grace and truth. Amen.

Epiphany
Ephesians 3:1-12

Fellow Heirs

Exegetical Aim: To explain the meaning of "heirs" in terms of salvation. Key verse: 6.

Props: Two sheets of paper with the word "Will" written across the top, a coffee mug, and a piece of jewelry.

Lesson: Good morning! Today I want to talk to you about something very important. Gather closely to me. Sometimes people own things that are very special to them. And if they die, they want their children to have those special things. So they decide to make what is called a "will." **Hold up the "will."** A will explains that certain things are to be given to others. The people that receive something from a will are called heirs. For instance, this is my coffee mug. **Hold up the coffee mug. Use two of the children to include in the will.** I could write in my will, "When I am no longer here, I want Joe to have my coffee mug." **Write on the piece of paper: Joe gets my coffee mug. Show them the will.** What does my will say? *(Joe gets my coffee mug)* **Hold up the jewelry.** Or, if I owned a piece of jewelry, I would write "Mary gets my jewelry." **Write this on the will.** Now what does my will say? *(Mary gets my jewelry)* Now, what would Joe and Mary be called? *(heirs)* They are heirs to my will. **Look at Joe and Mary and say,** I would give you my coffee mug and jewelry, but I'm not gone yet!

Application: Did you know that you are an heir to a really great fortune? The Bible says that we are fellow heirs of the promise in Jesus Christ. You are heirs! What do you think God has left us? *(response)* You think he has left us all coffee mugs and jewelry? *(response)* I don't think so. In fact he has left us his love, forgiveness, and a promise of eternal life. That's what he has left us. We will always be loved and we will live forever. What great gifts! The best thing is we don't have to wait for the gift. These things have already been given to us in Jesus Christ. **On the other "will" now write the words, love, forgiveness, and eternal life.** We are already loved by God, forgiven by God, and given eternal life through Jesus Christ. **Show them the new will and have them read it.** You are heirs of a very great fortune!

Let's Pray: Thank you, God, for making us your heirs and leaving us your love, forgiveness, and eternal life in Christ. Amen.

Baptism Of Our Lord
Luke 3:15-17, 21-22

God's Training Wheels

Exegetical Aim: To teach that baptism is a foundational event in the life of a Christian.

Props: Bicycle training wheels.

Lesson: Good morning. *(response)* What do I have in my hands? *(response)* How many of you have bicycles? *(response)* How old were you when you learned to ride? *(response)* Who taught you how to ride? *(response)* Before you learned to ride you had to use some special wheels. What were they called? *(training wheels)* That's right and these are training wheels. What would have happened, when you got on your bicycle for the very first time, if you had not had these? *(response)* You would have fallen. And, why would you have fallen? *(response)*

Application: Can you think of some other things that act like training wheels that keep us from falling? *(studying — learning the alphabet, practice — playing your scales)* What about in your Christian life? Are there things that act like training wheels? *(response)* Reading your Bible is like using training wheels. All of us — you, me, the minister, and your mom and dad — we all need God's help to keep us from falling and doing things that are wrong. Can you think of something other than the Bible that keeps us from falling? *(response)* Another thing that holds us up is baptism. Even Jesus himself was baptized. He received baptism because he wanted to be obedient to God. Some of you have already been baptized. We need to be baptized because that is another way in which God works in our life and helps us keep from falling. Sometimes I don't feel very close to God but then I remember: I was baptized into the family of God! I am his child.
 Hold up one of the training wheels: So I read the Bible and it helps support me on one side. **Hold up the other wheel:** And I

44

remember that I have been baptized into the family of God and that helps support me on the other. Those are two great training wheels.

Let's Pray: Dear Lord, hold me up and keep me from falling. Amen.

Baptism Of Our Lord
Acts 8:14-17

Laying On Hands

Exegetical Aim: To demonstrate the cleansing and unifying power of the Spirit.

Props: A very oily rag, and a container of mud.

Lesson: Good morning. Let me ask you a question. Before you came to church today, what did your mom or dad help you do? How did they help you get ready for church? *(response)* Right. They helped you get dressed with your nicest clean clothes. And you brushed your teeth and combed your hair. And you had a bath either this morning or last night. So they helped get you clean, didn't they? *(response)* Now that you are clean, I want to show you something. **Hold up the oily rag. Be careful not to let anyone touch it.** What is this? It looks awful, doesn't it? It's a rag that I use to clean up oil when I work on my car. All of you are so clean, do you think your moms and dads would want you to touch something that is unclean? Well, what about this? **Hold up the container of mud.** This is some mud that I found outside. Who wants to make some mud pies right here in church? *(response)* Do you think your moms or dads would want you to touch mud right now? *(response)* When things are dirty, we try not to touch them, right?

Application: In the days of Jesus, there were some people called Samaritans. And the Jewish people thought that they were dirty in the eyes of God. So they were not allowed to talk to or even touch a Samaritan. After Jesus went to heaven, he sent his Holy Spirit to anyone who would believe in him. And do you know what happened? The Holy Spirit came upon some Samaritans, the very people who were supposed to be dirty. But God had accepted them. Jesus' followers were in Jerusalem, and people were becoming Christians. The way they prayed for people who wanted to be Christians was by laying their hands on them. But there was a problem.

Were they supposed to touch the Samaritans? *(response)* But the Samaritans had received the Holy Spirit. So the disciples of Jesus went to the Samaritans, and do you know what they did? They went ahead and touched them anyway. They laid their hands on them and prayed. They decided that if God accepted them, then the Samaritans must not be dirty in his eyes after all.

Today we need to remember that there is no group of people in the world who are dirty in God's eyes. Sometimes when people are different from us we treat them like they are dirty, and we don't talk to them or get near them. But we should be willing to touch any persons and pray with and for them. People are not the same as an oily rag or a container of mud. God loves people and wants everyone to have his Spirit. And so all people should be loved by us, too, no matter who they are.

Let's Pray: Thank you, God, for loving all people. Help us to remember that no persons should be considered so unclean that we can't pray for them, touch them, or care for them. Amen.

Wine Into Water

Exegetical Aim: Miracles do not make a Messiah; the Messiah made miracles.

Props: A bottle of unopened grape juice and two clear glasses the same size. One glass should be filled slightly more than half way with liquid bleach which you will pretend is water. You will want a tray or a small firm table on which to put everything. Place the two glasses side by side.

Lesson: Good morning! *(response)* Has anyone ever been to a wedding? *(response)* Was it fun? *(response)* Why was it fun? What do you do at a wedding? *(response)* There is a lot of food and drinks. There's also a big cake and everybody is dressed up. Jesus went to a wedding once and there were a lot of people. So many people were there they ran out of wine. Wine was very important at weddings during Jesus' time. So everybody was standing around and they had run out. What do you think happened? *(response)* **If they don't know, don't answer yet.**

What do I have here? *(response)* Grape juice, that's right. Grape juice is a kind of wine. It's a brand new bottle so I will have to open it. **Pour the glass half full, and then take a drink to further prove it's grape juice. You will want the glass slightly less than half full.** So what do you think happened at the wedding when they ran out of wine? *(response)* Mary came up to Jesus and asked him to do something about it. And, Jesus went up to the jars which were full of water and he touched them. When he touched them, do you know what happened? *(response)* The water turned into wine? *(response)* How did that happen? **Point at the glasses:** It's like turning water into grape juice. How did he do that? *(response)*

Do you think we could do that this morning? Turn this water into grape juice? *(response)* I don't think that I could do that, but I think I might be able to turn the grape juice into water. Do you think I can do that? *(response)* You don't think so? **Pour the bleach into the glass with grape juice. It will turn clear.** What do you think about that? *(response)*

Application: Now don't ask me to turn it back into grape juice. I can't do that because what I did was a trick. But, Jesus didn't have to use tricks. He simply touched the water and it turned into wine. You know how he was able to do that? *(response)* It's because he was God. And God can do anything.

Let's Pray: Jesus, we know you can make miracles happen. You can take the water and make it red wine. You can take ours lives and make them shine. Amen.

Epiphany 2
1 Corinthians 12:1-11

Many Members, One Body

Exegetical Aim: To demonstrate the unity of the body of Christ.

Props: A hula hoop.

Lesson: Today I want us to play a game. It is called "Pass the Hula Hoop." Do you want to play? *(response)* Okay, let's stand up. Form a circle and join hands. **Place the hula hoop on one of the children's arms and then ask the children to form a circle holding hands. If there is not enough room for a circle, form a straight line.** The object of this game is to make the hula hoop go all the way around the circle, but you cannot let go of each other's hands. And you cannot touch the hula hoop with your hands. You have to wiggle your body and step through the hoop in order to pass it to the next person. Are you ready? Go! **Allow the children to wrestle with the problem. They will figure it out soon enough. Once the hoop has successfully passed around the circle a couple of times, have the children sit down.**

Did you like the game? *(response)* Good! Let me ask you a question about the game. What were the different things that you had to do in order to pass the hula hoop? *(jump, bend down, move the head, move the legs, etc.)* Did you do all of those things at once, or did you have to do them at different times? *(response)* Yes, different times. And if someone on the other side of the circle was passing the hoop, were you still doing something? *(response)* You were still holding on, and some of you gave encouragement to those who had the hoop. But you were still one group doing one task.

Application: In 1 Corinthians, the Apostle Paul reminded the Christians that the body of the church is one big body but it has many members. Your body has arms and legs and a head and feet. They don't do the same things, but they are still part of the same body. The same is true in your game. Not all of you did the same thing, but you were part of the same group. In the church, many people do different kinds of work, but we are all one church. Some people are good at encouraging others, some people pray, some people spread the word, some people help others a lot. But we are still part of the same church. All of you have something that you can do for the church. No matter what it is you can do, it is important. So I want you to think about what God wants you to do for the church. And remember to help others when they are doing what God wants them to do. Because the body is one and has many members.

Let's Pray: Thank you, God, for giving us the church. Thank you that you have given us different gifts to share with the church and for your sake. Amen.

Epiphany 3
Luke 4:14-21

Great Expectations

Exegetical Aim: Growing up and fulfilling a calling.

Props: None.

Lesson: Good morning! *(response)* I am going to ask your parents to help us. Let's turn around and look out at the congregation, and we are going to ask your moms, dads, and grandparents a question. Mom, Dad, what kind of person do you want your child to be when he or she grows up? Please stand up when you answer. **Allow all the parents to speak if possible. In larger churches you may want to arrange for three or four parents to state briefly their hopes and ask after the "planted" speakers if there are any others.**

Thank you, Mom, Dad, Grandma, and Grandpa. You can turn around now. Your parents have great expectations for you. They want you to grow up to be ... what? What did your parents say? *(honest)* What else? *(disciplined)* What else do they want you to be? *(caring)*

One day I hope you will fulfill their desires. One day Jesus stood up and announced that he was going to fulfill his Father's desires. He stood up in church **[the synagogue]** and said, "God's Spirit is upon me. I will give good news to the poor. I will bring freedom to prisoners. I will give sight to the blind."

Application: Jesus had grown up and he knew it was now time to fulfill his Father's desires. One day you will grow up and I pray you will try with all your heart, mind, soul, and strength to fulfill your parents' desires. Will you try to do that? *(response)* When you grow up I want you remember this day and the promise you made right here on these steps.

Let's Pray: Oh God, help these children to remember all their lives the promises that they make while they are young. Strengthen them to do good deeds and accomplish great things for you. Amen.

Epiphany 3
1 Corinthians 12:12-31a

A Body Strike

Exegetical Aim: To show that every member of the body is important.

Props: None needed.

Lesson: Let's play a game this morning. But for this game, I need a volunteer. *(response)* **Pick one child who you know will follow directions.** When I say, "Go," I want you to go over to the piano and then come back to this spot. Can you do that? *(response)* There's one other thing. While you are going, I'm going to tell you something else, and you have to do what I ask, okay?

Once upon a time there was a girl, and she decided to go see the church piano. **Instruct the child to walk very slowly toward the piano.** But while the child was going to see the piano ... she had to stop ... the child's feet decided that they didn't want to work anymore. The feet thought to themselves, "The arms and hands get more attention than we do, and it's just not fair." So they just quit working. **Instruct the child to act as though her feet quit working, and to sit down.** Now the child could not get to the piano. The rest of the body asked the feet to work, because the eyes wanted to see the keys on the piano. And the hands wanted to touch the keys, and the mouth wanted to sing a pretty song. But without the feet, the child could not go. Finally, the body begged the feet long enough and promised to pay more attention to the feet. So the child got up, went to the piano, and then came back home.

Application: Did you know that the Bible talks about the body that way? It asks what would happen if an eye decided to stop working, or if a hand didn't want to be a hand anymore. What do you think would happen? *(response)* That's right. The body could not function. In the same way, if we decide that we don't want to pray anymore, or we don't want to talk to others about Jesus, or that we don't want to give money anymore, what will happen to this body called the church? *(response)* That's right. The church would not work anymore. So it's very important that Christians always do what we are supposed to do. The whole church depends on us.

Let's Pray: Thank you, God, that you gave us something to do in the church. Thank you that we can pray, or share your love, or preach, or teach in your name. Amen.

Epiphany 4
Luke 4:21-30

The Truth Will Upset You
Before It Sets You Free

Exegetical Aim: We must listen to hard words as well as pleasant words. Notice the opposite reactions of the people in verses 22 and 28.

Props: None.

Lesson: Good morning! *(response)* All right. I want you to give me your reactions. When I say something you like I want you to yell, "Yea!" When I say something you don't like, I want you to whine, "But, Mom!" You got it? *(response)* You probably don't need any practice with this, but let's try it once. When it's something you like, you yell? *(yea!)* And when it's something you don't like, you whine? *(but, Mom)* Good, here goes:

> What do you say when your mom says, "Who wants to go to McDonald's?" *(yea)*
> What do you say when your mom says, "It's time for your bath." *(but, Mom)*

> What do you say when your mom says, "Who wants cookies?" *(yea)*
> What do you say when your mom says, "It's time for bed." *(but, Mom)*

> What do you say when your mom says, "Who wants to go to the movies?" *(yea)*
> What do you say when your mom says, "It's time to go to church." *(but, Mom)*

Well, what would happen if you never took another bath? *(response)* What would happen if you never went to bed? *(response)* And, what would happen if you never went to church again? *(response)* So you would be dirty, tired, and bad. So if you're dirty, tired, and bad, what kind of person are you going to be? *(response)*

Application: Jesus was speaking to a group of people one day and he said a lot of things that people liked. And they all said **motion to the children with your hands for them to respond,** *(yea!)* But then he said some things that were very true but the people didn't like what they heard, and the people said, *(but, Mom!)* Actually, it was, "But, Jesus." All those people grabbed hold of Jesus' arms and they took him to a hill and they were going to throw him down the hill, but he slipped out of their hands and escaped.

We are all smiles when nice things are said, but when hard things are said like, "Take a bath," or "Do your home work," we get all upset. Don't get upset when your mom tells you to do something that's good for you. It might be a little tough to do right now but you'll be better in the end for doing it. Next time your mom tells you: Time for your bath ... time for bed ... time for church, I want you to say **motion for them to respond,** *(yea!)* and tell her, "I don't want to be dirty, tired, and bad!"

Let's Pray: Lord, none of us wants to be dirty, tired, and bad. Help us to listen to you and obey you even when you ask us to do tough things. Amen.

Epiphany 4
1 Corinthians 13:1-13

Mirror, Mirror

Exegetical Aim: To show that though we do not understand everything now, one day God will show us all we need to know.

Props: A hand mirror.

Lesson: Today I have brought something to show you. **Hold up the mirror.** What is this? *(response)* Yes, it's a mirror. What do we use mirrors for? *(response)* We use them for a lot of things, don't we? We use them to look at ourselves, or to look behind us when we are in our cars. Sometimes when we are in a store, we will see mirrors in the corners of the aisle so that we don't accidentally bump into someone coming from the other way. We use mirrors for lots of things. But let me ask you something about the mirror. When I look in a mirror, do I see the same thing in the mirror as I do when I look with my eyes? *(response)* No, I don't. Everything in the mirror is reversed, so everything appears backward. And I can only see the things that are in the mirror, whereas my eyes can see much more. Let's do an experiment. I need two volunteers. **Pick two trustworthy children. Line the children one behind the other. Hold the hand mirror in front of the face of the person in front. Then ask the person in back to look into the mirror.** Now I will ask you to describe certain things about the person in front of you. But if you can't see it in the mirror, then you can't answer, okay? What color are the person's eyes? *(response)* What about the hair? *(response)* What color are the person's shoes? *(response)* **Mirror should be small enough not to reflect that far down.** Oh? You can't see the shoes? Here is another question. What does the back of this person's head look like? And remember, you have to use the mirror. *(response)* You can't see the back of the head with the mirror, can you? **Take the mirror down.** Now use your eyes. What color are the shoes? Is there anything on the back of the head? *(response)* Is it easier to use a mirror or to see face to face? *(response)* Yes, face to face.

Application: The Bible tells us in 1 Corinthians 13:12, "Now we see in a mirror dimly, but then face to face." Say that with me, "Now we see ... in a mirror dimly ... but then ... face to face." What do you suppose that means? *(responses, if any)* It means that even though there are things that we don't fully understand about God and heaven right now, one day we will know more fully. In our lives right now, we can only understand things just like looking in a mirror, because there are things that God can see that we can't see. When we are finally with God, we will understand things just like being face to face. So when you don't fully understand something, be patient. As we grow we learn more. And one day we will know more fully. So the next time you see a mirror, I want you to remember our Bible verse. Say it one more time, "Now we see in a mirror dimly, but then face to face."

Let's Pray: Thank you, Lord, that one day we will see you face to face, and we will understand things more at that time. In Jesus' name we pray. Amen.

Epiphany 5
Luke 5:1-11

Fishers Of Men

Exegetical Aim: The evangelistic nature of Christianity.

Props: A fishing pole or rod with no line.

Lesson: Two volunteers from the congregation to act like caught fish. The chairs of the evangelism committee and the outreach committee would be a good tie in. Otherwise, choose a male and female to represent the fish. I have a question for you this morning. What do I have in my hand? *(a fishing pole)* What do you do with a fishing pole? *(you catch fish with it)* That's right. How many of you have been fishing? *(response)* Did you catch anything? *(response)* What kind of bait did you use? *(response)*

There's a story about some men who went fishing. They fished all night and caught nothing. So they gave up and were putting their fishing nets away and they were disappointed. No fish after all that work!

What do you think happened next? Did they go home without any fish? *(response)* Why don't we see if we can catch some fish with this pole right now? Do you want to? *(response)* **Cast the imaginary line into the congregation. A volunteer will now jump up unexpectedly from the middle of a pew and be reeled in.** Oh, it's a big one! **When the fish arrives, take him off the "hook."** I'll just yank this out. **Have him sit down among the children.** Whew, that was exciting!

Well, those men didn't go home without any fish. Do you know why? *(response)* Because Jesus suddenly showed up, and Jesus told them to go out into the deep water and cast their nets one more time. And do you know what happened? They threw out their net **again another person from the other side of the congregation pops up in the middle of a pew and is reeled in** and they caught another fish. In fact, they caught so many fish in their net, the net began to break. **Introduce the two fish (committee members)**

60

and have them share what they do for the church. If they are not committee chairs, simply ask the two fish if they would like to follow Jesus. They are to respond, "Yes, we would."

Application: Jesus told these fishermen that they were no longer going to be fishing for fish but they were going to be fishing for people. This is how the church grows — by asking friends and neighbors if they would like to become followers of Jesus. You can do this too. You can be one of Jesus' fishermen. Let's go fishing for God and see if we can't catch some boys and girls. We can tell them that God loves them and ask them if they want to become followers of Jesus and join us here at church. Do that this week.

Let's Pray: Lord, teach us to be your fisherman ready to share your love with others. Amen.

Epiphany 5
1 Corinthians 15:1-11

Holding Fast

Exegetical Aim: To demonstrate the necessity of continually believing the gospel.

Props: A rope.

Lesson: How many of you are swimmers? *(response)* Good. Some of you can swim, and some of you will learn how one day. It's good to be in the water and to have fun when it is hot outside, isn't it? But sometimes we can get into trouble when we are swimming, can't we? If we get a gulp of water or a cramp, we can begin to sink in the water, and that's not good, is it? *(response)* **Hold up the rope.** What is this? *(response)* Yes. And for what might a rope be used if you are near people who are swimming? *(response)* Correct, it is something which can be held. If someone is in trouble and doesn't know how to swim, you can throw him a rope, and he can hold on to it to keep from sinking. You can save someone by throwing them a rope. What if that person decides that he doesn't need that rope anymore, and he lets go? What's going to happen? *(response)* Correct, he will sink.

Application: The Apostle Paul taught us how Jesus saves. Paul also said, "I would remind you of the gospel by which you are saved, if you hold it fast." The gospel of Jesus Christ is something that we have to hold onto every day of our lives. If we let go of the gospel of Jesus Christ, then we are going to begin to sink, aren't we? Jesus Christ died on the cross so that we might believe in him and be forgiven, and live life forever. Like a rope thrown out to us when we are sinking in water, we must hold on to the gospel of Christ that is given to us. So, never let go of the gospel of Christ. It is what saves you and me, if we hold it fast.

Let's Pray: Thank you, God, for sending your Son to save us from our sins. Help us always to hold fast to the gospel, because it is the gospel that saves us. Amen.

Epiphany 6
Luke 6:17-26

The Upside Down Cup

Exegetical Aim: The priorities of Kingdom living.

Props: A clear jar full of coins and a metal tray that will make lots of noise when struck by falling coins.

Lesson: Good morning! **With excitement and a positive tone:** Wouldn't it be great if we didn't have any money? I mean, if we were poor ... no money at all ... wouldn't that be great? *(response, if any)* Wouldn't it be great if we didn't have any food? If we went to bed tonight hungry ... wouldn't that be great! *(response)* Wouldn't it be great if we were crying now? I mean just having a good cry! Wouldn't that be great? *(response)* **wait for an actual response this time.** No? You mean that wouldn't be great? *(response)* Why? *(response)*

Raise the jar before the children with the tray underneath. What do I have in my hands? *(response)* That's right, it looks like a lot of money, doesn't it? What else can I put in this jar? *(response)* You mean I can't put anything else in the jar? *(response)* Why not? *(response)* What would happen if I were to turn this jar upside down? *(response)* **Incredulously:** No, they wouldn't fall out, would they? *(response)* No, I think it would be all right if I just turned it upside down a little bit, don't you? *(response)* **As you speak these next words turn the jar over causing a few coins to strike the tray:** I don't think anything will happen — **continue pouring** — oh, no! **Pour the coins slowly making as much racket as possible. Leave just a few coins in the jar.**

Application: While holding the jar before them say: Jesus says it would be good for you **shake the jar** if you are poor, because you will have the kingdom of God. He says it would be good for you to be hungry now, because you will be filled with goodness.

Jesus says it is good for you to cry because tomorrow you will laugh such a strong laugh. If we try to fill our lives with money and fill our lives with food and fill our lives with fun, fun, fun all the time — nonstop money, food, and toys, toys, toys — then we won't have time for the more important things in life.

Now there's some room in the jar. What are we going to fill it with? Can you tell me what the most important things in life are? **Let's hope they answer correctly.** *(response)* What are some more things that are very important? *(response)* Is money the most important thing? *(response)* Food? *(response)* Toys? *(response)* That's right. Let's fill the jar with God, Church, family, kindness to our school mates. Let's fill it with some love. **Optional: You might have some pieces of paper with these words on them and let the children place them in the jar as you say the words. If you do this, fold them and hand them to the children as they come forward. Let them read what's on the paper when you have emptied the jar of the coins.**

Remember. **Hold up the jar.** Jesus didn't say, "Fill our lives with money, pizza, and Barbie dolls." Jesus gave us two commandments: Love God with all your heart, and love one another with all your heart. Go and fill your jars as Jesus commanded.

Let's Pray: Lord, fill our lives with the good things of your kingdom. Amen.

Epiphany 6
1 Corinthians 15:12-20

First Fruits

Exegetical Aim: We all will experience eternal life.

Props: An apple.

Lesson: This morning I brought something to show to you. **Bring out the apple.** How many of you like apples? *(response)* What other kind of fruit do you like? *(response)* Fruit is good for us, so we should eat lots of it. I like apples, so I bought an apple yesterday. But then I got to thinking. Someone had to pick this apple in order for me to eat it. I started to wonder, if someone picks an apple off of the tree, does the tree die? *(response)* No? Why not? *(response)* What if it was the very first apple to appear on the tree? Will other apples still grow on the tree after I pick the first one? *(response)* Yes? Good! We can pick the first apple from a tree, but there will be a lot more to come. Many more apples will follow, because that's the way God made things. God will continue to provide beyond the very first fruits that are picked.

Application: Do you know what? That's the same way it is with eternal life. Jesus was the first to be raised from the dead forever, and he is now with God. Do you know what the Bible tells us about that? The Apostle Paul says, "In fact Christ has been raised from the dead, the first fruits of those who have died." He said that Jesus is like the first fruits. In the same way that more apples will follow the first one that is picked, Jesus was just the first who will be raised. Many more will follow. All who believe upon Jesus will enjoy eternal life with God, just like all of the other apples that will grow. Because that's the way God is. He will continue to provide beyond the first fruits. So the next time you see an apple, remember about the first fruit, and that Jesus is the first fruit of eternal life. And the promise of God is that we who believe will be the other fruit that follows.

Let's Pray: We thank you, God, that Jesus is the first fruit of eternal life. Help us to remember that you want us to join in that eternal life that Jesus brings. Amen.

Transfiguration
Luke 9:28-36 (37-43)

A Hearing Problem

Exegetical Aim: To teach the children the importance of listening.

Props: Your ears and fingers.

Lesson: While the children are getting into their position, stick your index fingers in your ears. Give them a moment to wonder what you're doing. After five seconds or so a child may say something to you but even if they don't, take away your fingers and look at one of the children who did not speak and say, "Did you say something?" *(no)* "Oh, okay." **Put your fingers back in your ears and ignore them again. Again the five seconds and the fingers out and say,** "I'm sorry, did you say something?"

As you say the following words, put your fingers back into your ears and leave them there. This time look at the children: I'm sorry, children, but lately I've had trouble hearing. I just can't hear a thing. *(response)* **If a child shouts at you, look directly at him, saying,** What did you say? Speak up! I can't hear you. You say I've got fingers? Well, of course, I've got fingers. They're in my ears. Oh, that's what you've been trying to tell me — I've got my fingers in my ears. Yes, I know, but that's beside the point. My problem is I haven't been hearing too well lately. *(response)* Take my fingers out and I will hear better?

Take your fingers out and look at the children. Oh, well, that does help. Thank you very much! You know sometimes it's hard to talk to people because they don't hear you. And it's not because they have their **hold your fingers up** fingers in their ears; it's because they don't want to listen. Has your mom or dad ever said to you, "Now, listen to me carefully"? *(response)* The next time they tell you to listen very carefully, do it, because they are going to say something very important.

68

Application: God rarely comes to earth and says, "Now, listen carefully," but he did that once. And when he said, "Listen carefully," he looked at us and pointed to his Son Jesus and said, "Listen, very carefully to him." We must do that throughout our lives. Your moms must listen to him; your dads must listen to him; I must listen to him and you must listen. Listen to Jesus very carefully. He always has something very important to tell us.

Let's Pray: Jesus, we are listening. We open our ears so that we might hear your teachings. Amen.

Transfiguration
2 Corinthians 3:12—4:2

Lifting The Veil

Exegetical Aim: To demonstrate that Jesus Christ shows us to God.

Props: A veil.

Lesson: How many of you have ever been to a wedding? At a wedding there are all sorts of neat things. What kind of things do you see or hear at a wedding? *(response)* Of course there are brides and grooms at weddings. The groom wears a nice suit or a tuxedo. And the bride wears a pretty dress. Many brides wear something on their faces. Do you know what it is called? *(response)* It is called a veil. **Hold the veil up for the children to see.** Here's one. I need a volunteer. **Choose a girl who volunteers, and demonstrate how the veil is worn.** Wow, that's really pretty. Let me ask you a question. Can you see very clearly now? *(response)* Lift the veil from over your eyes. Can you see better than when the veil was over your eyes? *(response)*

Application: The Apostle Paul teaches us something about Jesus, and he uses a veil to illustrate. He said that there are people who try to understand God without knowing Jesus Christ, and so they have a veil over their heads and are kept from understanding God. **Place the veil back over the eyes of the girl.** In other words, as hard as they try to see, they can't see clearly. But then Paul says, "Only through Christ is the veil taken away." Only in the life of Jesus do we see God clearly. If you want to know God fully, you must know Jesus, because he is the one who lifts the veil of our understanding. **Lift the veil from the eyes of the girl.** It is Jesus who lets us see God clearly. So the next time you are at a wedding and you see the veil over the bride's eyes, remember that it is Jesus Christ who lifts the veil of our understanding. It is Jesus who shows us God.

Let's Pray: Dear God, thank you for sending Jesus to show us your love most clearly. Thank you for letting us know you fully through Jesus Christ. Amen.

LENT

Lent 1
Luke 4:1-13

Wonder Bread

Exegetical Aim: The body is more than food.

Props: A loaf of bread (Wonder Bread if your region of the country sells it).

Lesson: Hold the loaf of bread before them. What do I have in my hands? *(response)* Can you tell me some of the things we make with bread? *(response)* That's right. What's your favorite thing you make with bread? *(response)* Peanut butter and jelly sandwich? That's my favorite too. What do we need in order to live? *(bread)* That's right, and why is bread important? *(response)* Bread is food, and we need food for energy. What else do we need in order to live? *(response)* **Possible answers are water, clothes, etc. Try to draw these ideas out of them, and talk to them about why these are important.**

If one of the children guesses early where you are headed, then use that thought for the following discussion. As important as food and water and clothes and houses are, we need more than this to live. Can someone tell me what else we need besides food, water, clothes, and a home? *(response)* **It will be great if you get something spiritually related but, if not, then suggest something.** Do we need our parent's love in order to live? *(response)* What about the lessons they teach us? *(response)* What kind of lessons do they teach you? *(response)* Do your parents teach you what an *A* and a *B* and a *C* look like? *(response)* What else do they teach you? *(response)* Do they tell you not to hit and not to tell any fibs? *(response)* You know we need to be taught how to behave.

73

Application: So, you see, we don't live by bread alone **hold up the bread** or by water alone. We also need to be taught how to live. We need to be taught to be kind and to tell the truth. Your moms and dads know this because God told them not to live by bread alone. They need to listen to God in order to live. It is God who tells us not to lie and to be kind to one another. You see, it takes a lot more than just bread to live. We need to listen to our parents, and we need to listen to God.

Let's Pray: Lord, give us your Word. We know that we cannot live simply by eating bread and food. We must have your Word to live. Amen.

Lent 1
Romans 10:8b-13

On Your Lips

Exegetical Aim: To show that the good news should always be on our lips.

Props: Some pennies (enough for each child to keep one) and a Polaroid camera.

Lesson: Today I want to show you a new game. It's called "Balance the Penny." Would you like to play? *(response)* **Hold a penny in your outstretched hand.** It's easy to balance a penny, don't you think? I'm doing it easily. Would you like to try? *(response)* **Give each child a penny, and instruct them to hold them very still in their hands.** Good job! You are balancing the penny. Okay, let's make it a little harder. Can you balance it on your index finger? **Demonstrate by placing the penny on the tip of your finger.** Good job! You can do that too. Okay, here's the hardest one. Now I want you to be very quiet for this one. Can you all close your mouths really tight? Can you balance the penny on your ... lips? Do like this. **Demonstrate, and encourage the children to do it. Once they have it, begin to talk to them again.** Keep balancing them. Don't stop, even though your faces are really funny right now. **While you are talking to them, reach over quietly and get out the Polaroid camera, then quickly take a picture of them with their funny faces. Now instruct the children to hold tightly to their pennies, and not to play with them anymore.** Wow, did you have funny faces with your lips sticking out and the pennies sticking out! **Let the children see the picture.**

Application: The Apostle Paul knew that if something was on our lips that it was easy to see. As a matter of fact, he said, "The Word is near you, in your heart and on your lips." Paul was saying that the words of Jesus should be on our lips. That way God's word will be easy to see. We should always be willing to tell people what we know about Jesus, so that they can see him. But some people just want to hold what they have. They grab hold of it and try to hide it, just like you are doing with your penny right now. No one can see or hear about Jesus from them. That's sad, isn't it? So where does God want us to put the words of Jesus? In our hands where no one can see them, or on our lips where everyone can see them? *(response)* Yes, on our lips. I want you to take the penny home with you, and whenever you see it, you can remember to keep the word of God on your lips.

Let's Pray: Thank you, God, for teaching us that we should always have your Word on our lips, and be willing to share the good news of Jesus with everyone. Amen.

Lent 2
Luke 13:31-35

A Father's Desire

Exegetical Aim: To communicate our Father's desire to gather and save his children.

Props: One of the newborn infants of the congregation or a baby doll.

Lesson: Hold the baby in your arms. What do I have in my arms? *(response)* Yes, and babies are very special. Can you tell me something that a baby needs? *(response)* **The children may need a little prompting here.** When a baby cries, what does the baby need? *(response)* And what else do they need when they cry? *(response)* Yes, they need food, and sometimes they need their diapers to be changed. When they are cold, what do they need? *(response)* When they are tired, what do they need to do? *(response)* When they are lonely, what do they need? *(response)* They need to be held and rocked. When they are dirty? *(bath)* When they are full of gas? *(burped)* Can you tell me anything else that a baby needs? *(response)*

Did your mom and dad do all these things for you? *(response)* Tell me some things they did for you? *(response)* Did they feed you? *(response)* How many times did they feed you? *(response)* Did they rock you and hold you? *(response)* How many times did they hug you and hold you? *(response)* Did they burp you, change your diaper, keep you warm, put you down for naps? *(response)* Why do you think your parents did all these things for you? *(response)*

That's right! When you were a baby, your parents wanted nothing else in all the world than for you to grow up to be big and strong like you are now. They loved you so much they did all these things for you. Not just once but over and over because you were their baby. Your mom and dad still feel that way about you.

Application: There is someone else who feels that way about you. Someone who wants to gather you in his arms and hold you and tell you how much he cares. Do you know who that is? *(response)* Your Father in heaven. Did you know that? That your Father in heaven loves you so much?

As long as you live, remember that! Whether you're a baby, a little girl or a little boy, a mom or a dad, a grandma or a grandpa, your heavenly Father wants to hold you and gather you all together and take care of you.

Let's Pray: Father, we thank you that you love us. We know you care for us, and, Father, we love you too. Amen.

Lent 2
Philippians 3:17—4:1

Imitating Goodness

Exegetical Aim: To teach that imitating what good people do is helpful.

Props: None needed.

Lesson: Good morning. Today I have a game for us to play. It's called the "Imitation Game." Would you like to play? *(response)* Okay, good! This is how you play. I will do something and then you imitate me. Ready? Here goes. **At this point do any simple movements such as touching your face or raising your hand, and let the children follow you.** You are really good imitators. Let me ask you a question, though. What if I were to burp really loudly right here during church? Would you still imitate me? *(you hope they will say no)* Why wouldn't you? *(response)* Right, because it's not a nice thing to do. But what if I were to shake hands with someone, **shake hands with one child,** would you imitate that? *(response)* Okay, ahead! **Let the children imitate the shaking of hands.**

Application: In the Bible, Saint Paul was a good man. And he told some early Christians this, "Join in imitating me." Why do you suppose he wanted the people to imitate him? *(response)* Yes, because he was good and he loved Jesus very much. Things that he did were worthy of imitating. If we imitate someone who is good, we do good things. If we imitate someone who is bad, we do bad things. Do you know who the Apostle Paul tried to imitate? *(Jesus)* Yes, he saw Jesus as his role model. Today I want you to think of ways to imitate Jesus. When you are about to eat, imitate Jesus. When you see someone feeling bad, imitate Jesus. When you are having a good time, imitate Jesus. When someone gives something to you as a gift, imitate Jesus. When someone asks you to share your toys, imitate Jesus. And after a while you will begin to be more like Jesus. And that will make God happy.

Let's Pray: Dear God, help us to imitate Jesus in everything we do, so that our lives may make you happy. Amen.

Lent 3
Luke 13:1-9

I'll Do Better Next Time

Exegetical Aim: To explain that God is patient with us when we don't live as we should.

Props: Crayons, a blank sheet of paper, and a little bit of artistic talent (but not much). On your sheet of paper draw a jumbled picture of a house, tree, and landscape, but make all the colors appropriate to the object. Draw the horizon. Put the roof's flat side on the horizon. Then on the tip of the roof, place the frame of the house upside down so that the door is up and the windows are down. You've got the picture now. Place the trees and birds in awkward places and draw the sun square. Draw a stick person walking on the sun. That should do it!

Lesson: Place the drawing face down. This morning, I want to show you a picture I drew. I'm really proud of it. I worked really hard. It's a picture of my house on a sunshiny day. I mean it's got sunshine, a pretty house, trees, and birds in it. You want to see it? *(response)* **Show the children the drawing.** Isn't this great! *(response)* Do you like it? *(response)* What? *(response)* No, no, no, there's nothing wrong here. Here's my roof on the ground. *(response)* Doesn't the roof belong on the ground? *(response)* It doesn't? Where does it belong? *(response)* Okay, I'll remember that. The roof belongs on the top of the house. I'll do better next time.

Well, what about the sun? It's just shining! *(response)* What? *(response)* **While they are shouting out it's square or it's supposed to be round, continue with your thoughts.** I don't understand. *(response)* **Interrupt them.** No, look, it's shining nice and bright and making the grass grow. *(response)* What's wrong? *(response)* You mean, it's not supposed to be square? *(response)* It's supposed to be round? *(response)* Okay, I'll remember that. The sun is supposed to be round. I'll do better next time.

Well, this one is neat. This is me up here walking on the sun. *(response)* What? *(response)* You mean this is wrong too? *(response)* I got it all wrong, didn't I? *(response)*

Okay, I need to remember this. **Point to the objects as you remember your corrections.** The house goes under the roof and the roof on top of the house. And I'm not supposed to be walking on the sun. That's all wrong. I need to be down here on the grass. And the next time I draw the sun, I need to make it round not square. I'll do better next time.

Application: Sometimes we do get things all mixed up in life. Do you ever fight with your friends? *(response)* Have you ever been stingy and refused to share with your brother or sister? *(response)* Did you know that from time to time your mom and dad get things all mixed up and they get mad at each other? *(response)* When we fight and say bad things, our lives are all mixed up **hold up the drawing** like my picture. We need to do better.

I want you to know that God loves us all and is patient with us. And when we fight and act ugly, he is waiting for you and me to straighten up our lives. Now I will remember to put the roof and the sun and the little stick person in the right places next time. And I want you to remember not to fight with one another, not to be ugly, and to do as God asks: to love one another.

Let's Pray: Father, we make mistakes so we ask for your forgiveness, but help us all to do better next time. Amen.

Lent 3
1 Corinthians 10:1-13

A Tempting Offer

Exegetical Aim: To communicate God's love for us as he tells us to guard against temptation.

Props: Hershey's Kisses and a plate.

Lesson: Bring out the candy in a bag. Tell the children that you have something for them, and then pour the candy out on the plate, slowly. I have something for us to see this morning. What are these? *(response)* Yes, they are Kisses. Don't touch them! Let me just pour them out. Don't touch them! **Sit and stare. After a few seconds, say again,** No one touch them. **Again stare longingly at the candy. You might even sigh and say,** I sure would like some candy. **As they giggle or lose composure, say,** Would you like to eat the candy? *(response)* I would too but do you know why we can't have the candy right now? *(because we're in church)* Yes, we can't eat the candy now because it's not the appropriate time to do so. Sometimes we see things that look very good to us, but it's not always the best thing for us. When your mom tells you that you can't do something or you can't have something, you don't know why, but she knows why. She sees things you cannot see.

Application: In the same way, God our Father loves us very much and wants us to stay away from temptations. We need to stay away from temptations like being mean to people even when they are mean to us. Or if someone is breaking the rules at school and wants us to join along, we need to do what? *(response)* Right, we need to walk away and not do that. So you see, we might want to do something, but it may not be the best thing to do. You need to listen to your mom and dad who know best. No matter how disappointed you may be, remember, your parents are wise, and God is even wiser than we.

83

Let's Pray: Thank you, God, for loving us. Help us to stay away from temptations and to do only what you want us to do. In Jesus' name. Amen.

Allow the children to take one piece of candy to their seats, instructing them that they may eat it after church.

Lent 4
Luke 15:1-3, 11b-32

Lost And Found

Exegetical Aim: To convey the joy that occurs when that which was lost is found.

Props: Your wristwatch that you will hide somewhere close.

Lesson: Good morning! *(response)* Well, we all made it to church this morning, didn't we? *(response)* What time did you have to get up in order to make it to church on time? *(response)* I wonder what time it is right now. Does anyone know how to tell time? *(response)* **If there is a child who knows how or says he/she does, ask that child:** So if I showed you my watch, you'd be able to tell me the time? **Raising your hand to show the child your watch, you are surprised.** What? Where is my watch? Oh, no! I've lost my watch. Where did it go? We've got to find my watch. Will you help me look for it? Get up and help me find it.

  As you act like you are looking for it, repeat several times "I've lost my watch. It's lost! It's lost!" **If no child can find the watch, guide them.** I think I might have lost it somewhere over here. Will you help me look over here?

  When it is found, go back to the usual meeting place: Thank you for helping me find my watch. I am really relieved. **If the watch has a special sentimental value, explain why losing the watch would hurt.** Have you ever lost anything? *(response)* What did you lose? *(response)* How did you feel when you finally found it? *(response)* Yes, you felt just as I did when my watch was found. You felt happy and joyful because what was lost is now found. You lost [name one of the children's lost items]. How did you feel when you found it? *(response)* That's right; you felt happy and joyful.

Application: It's easy to lose things like watches and toys. But sometimes even we can get lost. **Briefly and with the basic elements, tell the story of the Prodigal Son (e.g. wonderful**

home, ran away, ran out of money, got hungry, came back home, begged to be let back in, and the Father hugged and kissed him, bringing him back into the family). He remembered that his Father loved him — that he had a home and food and warm clothes. Sometimes we run away from God and we need to find our way back home. So you see, it's not only watches **show them your watch** that can get lost; we can get lost. And God is joyful and happy when we pray to him and ask him to forgive us.

Let's Pray: Lord, when we come back home to you, we know that you will be waiting. Amen.

Lent 4
2 Corinthians 5:16-21

Ambassadors For Christ

Exegetical Aim: To demonstrate that Christians are to be ambassadors for God's kingdom.

Props: One child who is a "plant." Before the children's sermon, you have spoken to this child and he/she is instructed on what to do at the appropriate time.

Lesson: Who would like to play a game? *(response)* What's your favorite game? *(response)* I would like to teach you a game today. The name of my game is the "Ambassador Game." Do you know what an ambassador is? An ambassador is someone who represents his country to another. And the only things that the ambassador can officially say about his country are the things that his country wants him to say. The "Ambassador Game" is like "Follow the Leader," but it has one difference. I'm going to tell you something to do, and you have to do it. But the only way that you will know what I want you to do is through another person. That person will be my ambassador. Are you ready to try? *(response)* Okay.

Pick out one person to be your ambassador and tell the rest of the children to do exactly what he tells them to do. Whisper to your ambassador: Stand up and bend over and touch your toes. *(they touch their toes)* Great job. I told [Child's name] to tell you to touch your toes, and that's exactly what happened. She is a good ambassador. **Choose another ambassador. Whisper to your ambassador:** Flap your arms like a bird. *(they flap their arms)* Great job. I told [Child's name] to tell you to flap your arms like a bird, and that's exactly what happened. He is a good ambassador.

Now I need another ambassador. **This time, choose your "plant" to be your ambassador. Your plant has been previously told to tell the children to jump up and down. Whisper:** Rub your heads. *(response)* Wait a minute. That's not what I told him to tell you. **Ask the ambassador:** What did I ask you to tell them to do? *(response)* He was not my ambassador, because he didn't do as I asked. Now I want you to know that [Child's name] was just helping me, and he didn't really mess up. Before we met today I asked him to help me. But you can see how important it is for an ambassador only to say the things that the country who sends him wants him to say.

Application: In the Bible, the Apostle Paul tells us that we are to be ambassadors for Christ. What do you suppose that means? *(response)* It is very important for us to do exactly as Christ wants us to do and say what Christ wants us to say. If we don't do what God wants us to do, then we are not being good ambassadors for Christ. But when we do as he says, to love God and love one another, then we are being good ambassadors for Jesus.

Let's Pray: Thank you, God, for letting us be ambassadors for you. Help us always to do what you want, so that we will be the best ambassadors possible. Amen.

Lent 5
John 12:1-8

A Great Party

Exegetical Aim: Honoring Jesus.

Props: A bottle of fine perfume and a piece of 8.5 x 11 paper.

Lesson: How many of you have ever been to a party? *(response)* What kind of a party was it? *(response)* What did you do at the party? *(response)* Parties are a lot of fun, aren't they? *(response)* Have you ever been to a party where someone was being honored? *(response)* Maybe it was their party because they were 100 years old. Or maybe they had just had a baby. Or maybe they had done something really great. Have you ever been to a party because someone had done something really great? *(response)* **You may not get a response, but give them just a moment to think about it.** What did they do that was great? *(response)*

Jesus went to a party that was in his honor; he did something fantastic. Do you know what he did that was so great? He raised somebody from the dead! I mean, this guy — his name was Lazarus — this guy had been dead for four days and he had already been buried. And Jesus went to the place where he was buried and said, "Lazarus come out of that grave!" And guess what happened? *(response)* That's right. He came back to life. That's great, isn't it? *(response)*

Now who do you think was throwing this party for Lazarus? *(response)* It was Lazarus' sister, Martha. She was so happy that Jesus had raised her brother from the dead that she threw a party for Jesus.

Application: What do I have in my hand? *(response)* That is right. It is perfume. When Jesus was at this party, a lady named Mary came up to Jesus and she had a bottle of perfume in her hand. She knelt down in front of Jesus and put perfume on his feet. **Splash a healthy amount of perfume onto the piece of paper so it wafts**

89

by the children. Then she began to dry his feet with her long hair. What a beautiful thing to do. **Now, as you speak, pause a bit and move the paper around the inner circle of the children to produce a strong scent (verse 3b: And the house was filled with the fragrance of the perfume).**

You see, this was Jesus' party and Mary knew that Jesus had done a great thing, but as wonderful as that was — raising Lazarus from the dead — Jesus was going to do something even greater. What do you think he was going to do? *(response)* Jesus was going to die and he would be dead and buried for three days and then God would raise him from the dead. And, the great things is, he will never, never die again. And he promises that you and I will be with him. In fact, we are all going to this big party. We call this great party heaven. You will be there and I will be there and your mom and dad will be there. How great that will be!

Let's Pray: Lord, we honor you this morning and look forward to a great party one day when we shall all be together. Amen.

Lent 5
Philippians 3:4b-14

The Prize

Exegetical Aim: To demonstrate the importance of persistence.

Props: A trophy of some sort. Adapt this sermon to the type of trophy that you have.

Lesson: Good morning! I want to show you something that is very important to me. **Hold up the trophy.** What is this? *(response)* Yes, it's a trophy. Can you tell from the little person on top of the trophy what I did to receive the trophy? *(response)* Yes, that's right. It's for playing basketball. But it wasn't easy. Have any of you ever played a sport, or been in dancing class, or gotten good grades in school? *(response)* Many of you, I see. Well, was it easy? Or did you have to work hard and practice so that you could do the best you could do? *(response)* Yes, practice is a part of playing any sport or doing anything that's important. Let me ask you something. If you are playing a sport, can you do anything you want or do you have to play by the rules? *(response)* Yes, you have to play by the rules. When do you get a trophy? Before you start the games, or after all of the games are over? *(response)* Correct, you receive it after the games have been played. Do you get the trophy if you quit after the first game, or do you have to practice every day and play all the games and make it to the end of the season? *(response)* Right, you have to make it all the way through. That's the purpose of the trophy. That's why they are special. They remind us that we have played by the rules and worked hard to achieve something important.

Application: Saint Paul said the same thing about being a Christian. He said that as a Christian, he was pressing on toward the goal for his prize. He meant that as a Christian, he was going to play by the rules. What book contains the rules for a Christian? *(response)* The Bible, yes. He said he was going to work hard and practice every day being a Christian. What are things that a Christian should do? *(response)* What are some things we could do every day to make us better at these things? *(response)* Paul also said he would one day receive his trophy. What is the trophy for a Christian? *(response)* Yes, heaven. One day, our jobs as Christians will be through here. But if we have been faithful, if we haven't quit, if we've practiced hard, if we have the Bible and believed in Jesus Christ, then we will receive the trophy of life from God. So the next time you see a trophy, remember to be faithful in your life with God.

Let's Pray: Gracious God, thank you for promising not to forget us. Keep us faithful, so that we might receive the trophy of heaven when all is through. In Jesus' name. Amen.

Palm Sunday
Luke 19:28-40

The Candy Cane

Exegetical Aim: To show how God can be within our midst and we can fail to recognize him (this appears to be Luke's Triumphal Entry theme, key verse: 42b).

Props: A traditional candy cane or any candy cane with red stripes. If you cannot find one, draw it.

Lesson: Good morning! **Open the candy cane and start eating it or just hold it before them.** Mmmm! This is a really good candy. **Eat some more.** Now, what is this I'm eating? *(response)* That's right; it is a candy cane. You know it takes a long time to eat a candy cane. What do you like most about a candy cane? *(response)* Yes, it is sweet and fun to eat. In fact, it's not just candy; it's a reminder. The candy cane is about someone's life.

It's really a unique candy. **Hold the candy before them.** A candy man in Indiana made the first candy cane. He made it because he wanted to remind us of someone. I want you to figure out who. First, he made a plain white peppermint stick. Do you know why the candy man made it white? *(response)* Because, the color white is a symbol for purity and goodness. Then, he added three small stripes. Can you see the three small stripes? **Bring the cane closer. You will have to use your own discretion here as to the use of the following ideas with the children.** The small stripes remind us that this person was beaten up badly. Next, the candy man put a big red stripe on it because this person was hurt so badly that he started bleeding. The candy man's fourth hint is the shape of the candy cane. Can you tell me what this looks like? *(response)* It's a shepherd's staff. This person is our shepherd. He looks after us. The last hint is this **turn the cane upside down.** What letter of the alphabet is this? *(j)* That's right it's a "J." Whose name begins with "J"? *(Jesus)* It's so much fun to eat, we forget there is a story behind the candy cane. It reminds us of Jesus.

Application: So next time you are having fun eating the candy cane, remember the story: **Hold the cane in its respective positions and point out the symbols as you say:** Jesus was pure and good like the white; he was hurt badly on the cross and bled like the red stripes — three stripes for his pain and one big one for his blood; and he did all this for us because he's our shepherd.

Let's Pray: Lord, we remember your life and how you suffered for us. Amen.

Palm Sunday
Philippians 2:5-11

I Know What You Want

Exegetical Aim: Teaching the importance of having the mind of Christ.

Props: Two puppets. Give them any names you want.

Lesson: As the children gather, tell them the names of the puppets. The puppets want to tell you a story. Once upon a time there were two children and they were the best of friends. Every day they would walk down the street and see pretty trees and wave to the birds and say hello to their friends. **Act all of this out with the puppets as you tell the story.** And the favorite part of the walk for them was going to the ice cream store. 'A' would say, "I want vanilla," and 'B' would say, "I want chocolate." **Give different voices to the puppets as they order the ice cream.**

The next day they went down the street. **Retell the story, until the characters go into the ice cream store.** 'A' said, "Today, I want raspberry," and 'B' said, "I want chocolate."

Tell the story again, until they get into the ice cream store, with 'A' ordering orange sherbet, and 'B' ordering chocolate again. Maybe this time, let the children answer for 'B.'

Once more through the story, with 'A' ordering pistachio, and by now all of the children will order chocolate ice cream for 'B.'

Application: How did you know that was what B was going to say? *(response)* Yes, that's correct. When we know someone well, we begin to know what they are thinking. And you knew exactly what B was thinking. Do you know what the Bible says? It says that we ought to have the mind of Christ. And that means that we should get to know Jesus so well that we begin to know what he wants us to do. Jesus always wants us to serve other people, and to be nice to those around us, and to love God at all times. The more you know Jesus, the more you will know what he wants. We are to have the mind of Christ.

Let's Pray: Dear God, help us to know our Lord better, so that we will know his mind and what is best for us. Amen.

EASTER

Easter
John 20:1-18

I Can't Believe It

Exegetical Aim: Things are not always as they seem.

Props: A large transparent bowl and an egg carton full of eggs (one of which is hard boiled).

Lesson: Place the bowl in the middle of the children on the floor and hold the carton of eggs in your hands. Good morning. *(response)* Does anyone know what day this is? *(response)* That's right; it is Easter. And what do we celebrate on Easter? **A few of them may know the answer. Some may need help.** On Good Friday we remember that Jesus died and he was dead for three days in a grave. Today, Easter, we remember he came back to life. We call this the resurrection of Jesus. We also call it Easter.

A lady named Mary was there on the very first Easter when Jesus came back to life. She went to the garden and she met a man there. She thought he was the gardener. But who was he really? *(response)* Then Jesus called her by her name. He said, "Mary." And Mary suddenly realized that it was Jesus. She couldn't believe her eyes; he was alive!

What do I have in my hand? *(response)* I took this out of the refrigerator this morning and brought it here to church to show you something. **As you talk to the children slowly take the hardboiled egg out of its carton as if it is a fresh egg. Show them the egg.** Is this an Easter egg? *(response)* No, it's not, is it? It's not colored like an Easter egg. Did anyone find any Easter eggs this weekend? *(response)* How many did you find? *(response)* **Holding the egg a couple inches from the bottom of the bowl.** What would happen if I dropped the egg from here? *(response)* **Hold it a couple of feet above the bowl.** What would happen if I dropped it from here? *(response)* **Hold it high above your head.** What would happen if I dropped it from here? *(response)* **Stand up and hold the egg above your head.** What would happen if I dropped it from here? *(response)*

Everyone scoot up to the bowl. **They will probably all jump back. Surprise them by dropping the egg.** What happened? *(it's hard-boiled)* **Bend down with the children and examine the egg with them.** What did you think was going to happen? *(it was going to splatter on everything)* You thought it was a fresh egg. You didn't know it was hard-boiled.

Application: Things are not always as they seem. Mary saw Jesus die. So when she saw him in the garden, she thought he was the gardener. When you saw the egg, you thought it was fresh. It took you a little while to understand it was hard-boiled.

When something incredible happens, like Jesus being raised from the dead, it's hard to believe. It takes a little while for us to understand. Remember: he was dead but he is risen!

Let's Pray: Oh, Lord, you are no longer dead. You are alive. It's hard to believe, but it's true! Amen.

Easter
1 Corinthians 15:19-26

Protective Authority

Exegetical Aim: To demonstrate that everything is under the authority of Christ.

Props: Safety glasses, gloves, lip balm, soap, toothpaste, or anything that can be used for protection, and a bag to hold the items.

Lesson: Today, I want to share with you some things of mine that I use to keep from getting hurt. I will show an item to you, and you tell me how it protects me. Okay? *(response)* **Hold up the safety glasses.** What are these? *(response)* From what do these protect me? *(response)* Very good, that's right. These protect my eyes from dust or other objects. **Ask the child who answers to hold that object. Follow the same pattern for each of the other items: Gloves protect us from the cold, lip balm from the wind, soap from germs, toothpaste from cavities, etc.**

Application: There are lots of other things in the world that we can use for protection. But do you know what the best protection in the world is? Jesus Christ. The Bible says, "God has put all things under [Jesus'] feet." Do you know what that means? *(response)* When something is under your feet it is under your control, isn't it? So if everything is under the feet of Jesus, who is in control? *(response)* We who have faith in Christ have nothing to fear, do we? If you are picked on or called names, or scared in a storm, or whatever it may be, just remember that you don't need to be frightened or sad. Jesus can be your protection.

Today is Easter, when Jesus defeated death and came back to life. Because of that, Jesus is more powerful than anything. So he can help you with any problem that you have. You can always go to him and find strength. Because everything is under his feet, Jesus has authority over all.

Let's Pray: Dear God, we thank you that you have given your Son Jesus Christ authority over the world so that he protects us. Amen.

(Special thanks to Dick Reed of Drummonds, Tennessee, for this idea.)

Easter 2
John 20:19-31

I Doubt It!

Exegetical Aim: Thomas' transition from doubt to faith concerning the resurrection of Jesus.

Props: A talent that will come as a surprise to the children; e.g., being able to juggle. You must be able to perform the talent before the children. If you use the object it needs to be hidden until revealed. A unique object could be used rather than a talent.

Lesson: Good morning. *(response)* I have a talent that none of you know about. Do you want to know what my talent is? *(response)* I don't think you are going to believe me, but I can juggle. *(response)* **As you say "juggle," show them the balls and drop them into the crowd of children. This will create doubt in the minds of the children.** What? You don't think I can juggle? *(response)* I can see that some of you doubt I can do it. Well, I've brought these three tennis balls and I am going to prove to you that I can juggle, but I'm only going to show a few of you. I want you to turn around and cover your eyes. Turn around. Now, you can't turn around until I say so, and no peeking, so I want you to cover your eyes.

At this time perform the talent being watchful of peekers. Okay, everyone can turn around. You didn't think I could do it, did you? *(response)* But do you believe I can do it now? *(response)* **Address the congregation:** They didn't see me do it. Could you tell them I did it? *(response)* **Now ask if they believe.** Now do you believe I can do it? *(response)*

She doesn't believe that I can juggle; so, I want you to turn around and cover your eyes. I am going to do it one more time. **Perform the talent a second time.** Okay, you can turn around. Now do you believe I can juggle? *(response)* **You hope the response will be, "No."** Why not? *(response)* **Usually the children will say, "We have to see it."**

101

Perform the event or show the object. Now do you believe? *(yes)*

Application: This is exactly what happened after Easter. Jesus appeared to all the disciples except Thomas, and Thomas couldn't believe it. Everybody tried to tell Thomas that Jesus was alive, but he wouldn't believe. He said, "Unless I see it with my own two eyes and touch him with my own hands, I am not going to believe." And guess what? *(response)* Jesus appeared again to the disciples and this time Thomas was there. Thomas saw Jesus with his own two eyes and touched him with his own two hands and then Thomas believed. Then Jesus said something wonderful. He said, "Thomas, you have believed because you have seen; blessed are those who have not seen me and yet still believe in me." Do you know who Jesus was talking about? *(response)* He was talking about you and me. We did not see Jesus after the resurrection but we still believe.

Let's Pray: Lord, we did not see you when you were raised from the grave, so sometimes we have doubts. But, Lord, we believe you are alive! Amen.

Easter 2
Revelation 1:4-8

A To Z

Exegetical Aim: To demonstrate that Jesus is the Lord of all, the first and the last.

Props: Large cutouts of the letters *A* and *Z* and cutouts of the Greek letters *Alpha* and *Omega*.

Lesson: How many of you know the alphabet? *(response)* Okay, good. How many of you know what the five vowels are? *(response)* Good, you are smart! What about this question: What are the two middle letters of the alphabet? *('m' and 'n')* Good. Let's try this one: What is the very first letter of the alphabet? *(response)* Exactly! It is *A*. **Hold up the letter *A*.** Okay, what is the very last letter of the alphabet? *(response)* Yes, it is *Z*. **Hold up the letter *Z*.** So, if I hold these two letters together, what am I representing by the *A* and the *Z*? *(response)* Right. The alphabet. Everything is in between the *A* and the *Z*. All of the vowels, consonants, the middle letters, everything. All of the words that we use, all of the words in the Bible, and everything that we are taught comes in between the letters *A* and *Z*. **Hold up the Greek letters.** Does anyone know what these are? These are Greek letters, the Alpha and the Omega. Say that with me, Alpha *(alpha)* and Omega *(omega)*. For people in the time of Jesus, it was the same as our *A* and *Z*. Everything was in between the Alpha and the Omega.

Application: In the Bible, Jesus told John that he is the Alpha and the Omega. What do you think he was saying? *(response, if any)* Jesus was saying that he is the beginning of this world and the end of this world. He is the beginning of your life and the end of your life. He existed before the world and he will be alive after the world ends. He is greater than all of this world because he is the Son of God. If that's so, then Jesus can handle all of the good things and

103

the bad things that happen to us. So I want you to remember always that Jesus is the Alpha and the Omega, the first and the last. Say that with me one more time, the Alpha and the Omega *(alpha and omega)*, the first and the last *(the first and the last)*. The next time you see an *A* or *Z*, remember that Jesus surrounds you in his love and care, from the beginning until the end!

Let's Pray: Dear Father, thank you for sending your Son Jesus Christ to surround us with his love. Thank you that we do not have to worry about our lives because Jesus Christ is surrounding us from the beginning to the end. Amen.

Easter 3
John 21:1-19

You Have To Work At It

Exegetical Aim: The effort involved in loving God and one another.

Props: None. This sermon may need some adaptation if you have a large sanctuary; however, the sermon is designed to create commotion within the congregation and the closer to which this is allowed the better the effect. Especially if the reading of John 21:1-19 or 15-19 immediately follows.

Lesson: When the children are settled: I have a question for you this morning, "Do you love your mom and dad?" *(response)* **Get as many children to answer as possible.** If you love them, I want you to go to them and hug them and come right back. If your mom or dad is not here, then go hug the person who brought you here. **As the children return and are getting settled:** I have another question for you, "Do you truly love your mom and dad?" *(response)* Then, I want you to go to them and hug them and come right back. **If they pause and look at you a bit dumb-founded, urge them on.** Go on! **As they return and before they get settled again:** Now wait, before you sit down I've got one more question for you, "Do you really really love your mom and dad?" *(response)* Then, I want you to go hug your mom and dad and come right back.

Application: You may sit down this time. I wanted to make sure that you really did love your mom and dad. It's not enough just to hug them once. Loving takes a lot of work. Was that hard work? Going three times, hugging three times, and coming back? *(response)* Really loving people is hard work. Every day we need to tell our mom and dad and our sisters and brothers how much we care for them. Tomorrow, sometime, when you're playing with your toys, stop what you're doing and go find your mom or your dad and hug them. Will you do that? *(response)* Good! Let's put some work in our love.

Let's Pray: Dear Lord, help us to work hard at loving one another. Amen.

Easter 3
Acts 9:1-6 (7-20)

A Chosen Vessel

Exegetical Aim: To show that God uses unlikely people for his work.

Props: A designer vase with a small mouth, one very plain (maybe even ugly) vase with a larger mouth, and a number of wrapped flowers that can only fit in the plain container (because of the size of the bouquet).

Lesson: I have some very nice things to show you this morning. What are these? **Show the vases.** *(response)* **Pick up the designer vase.** This vase is very pretty, isn't it? What do you see on the vase? *(response)* **Discuss the intricacies of the vase, and tell a story of its meaning to the family, or of something that gives it value. Now pick up the plain vase.** Do you like this vase? *(response)* No, it's not as pretty as the first one.

Now pull out the flowers. When your dad gives flowers to your mom — and that does happen, doesn't it? *(response)* — or when you pick her some flowers, in what does she put the flowers? *(response)* A vase kind of like this one. What else does she put in the vase? *(response)* That's right, flowers can't survive without water. Well, we need a very special place to put our flowers — in which vase do you think your mom would put the flowers? *(one hopes most children will pick the designer vase)* **Try putting the flowers in.** They won't fit! What are we going to do? Oh, you think they'll fit in this vase? *(response)* But it's so plain. *(response)* Well, what do you know! They fit perfectly. That doesn't look so bad after all.

Application: It turns out that the best container for the flowers was the one that no one wanted to choose. Something similar happened to Saint Paul. He was someone that Christians didn't trust, and many didn't like him. But God chose him to be a special carrier of the message of Christ. God has a way of using anybody who wants to serve him. It doesn't matter if you are the strongest, or the smartest, or the prettiest. What does matter is that you love God, and know that God can use you. So, if this plain container can carry these beautiful flowers, and if Saint Paul can be a messenger of God's word, so can God use any of us to tell his message and carry his love to other people.

Let's Pray: God, thank you for making us the way we are, and thank you for using us to carry your message no matter who we are. We love you. In Christ's name we pray. Amen.

Easter 4
John 10:22-30

My Cup Overflows

Exegetical Aim: To demonstrate how God lavishes upon us his goodness and grace. Key verses: 28 specifically and Psalm 23:5b.

Props: A full pitcher of water, a good size clear glass, and a pan large enough to hold the water that will make ample noise when struck by falling water.

Lesson: Good morning! *(response)* How many of you this morning have friends? *(response)* Could anyone tell me why friends are important? *(response)* How many of you have brothers and sisters? *(response)* Tell me why brothers and sisters are important. *(response)* How many of you have moms and dads and grandparents? *(response)* Why are moms and dads so important? *(response)* Now, we've come to the best question. Tell me why grandparents are so important. *(response)* It's good to have all these people around because they add so much to our lives.

Place the pan in the middle of the children and hold the glass over the pan. As you say these next words, fill the glass approximately one-tenth full: Friends add **pour the water** so much to our lives. We play games with them. **Bring attention to the glass.** We talk with them and have all kinds of fun. Brothers and sisters are also important because they are part of our family. They add **now pour another tenth** even more to our lives. They love us and share their toys with us. They're always there to talk to; sometimes, they can teach us how to do new things. Moms and dads add **now pour two-tenths or one-fifth more** such a great deal to our lives it's hard to count how many things they do for us. They feed us and teach us; they love us and bathe us; they put bandaids on our boo-boos and hold us and rock us to sleep. They add so much to our lives! And what about your grandparents? Wow, they add **pour another fifth so that the glass is three-fifths full** so much to our lives. Grandparents buy us candy, don't they? *(response)* And they take us neat places and they love it best when we crawl up in their laps and fall asleep on their shoulders. And Grandma makes the best brownies! Grandparents are really special.

Application: For all that our friends, brothers, moms, dads, and grandparents do for us, they can only give us so much. They can't completely fill our cup. Only God can fill our cups. And, you know something, when God gives **now fill the glass at a very slow and steady pace as you complete this paragraph** he keeps giving and he never stops. He adds **let the glass overflow at the same rate until all the water is poured out of the pitcher** so much to our lives. He gave you your life and fills it with sunshine and rain; he fills it with friends and family. And, he doesn't stop there. He protects us and watches over us. He fills us with goodness and mercy. And, one day, we will live for ever and ever with God and our friends and family. God is so good! He fills our cups to overflowing!

Let's Pray: Lord, our cups are filled to overflowing because of your great love for us. We cannot contain all that you give. Amen.

Easter 4
Revelation 7:9-17

No More Tears

Exegetical Aim: To show that in heaven there will be no tears.

Props: A bottle of baby shampoo and some Kleenex tissues.

Lesson: How many of you have ever washed your hair? *(response)* Good, all of you have washed your hair before. **Hold up the bottle of baby shampoo.** Did your mom or dad ever use baby shampoo to wash your hair? *(response)* Why did they use baby shampoo? *(response)* Because if baby shampoo gets in your eyes, it doesn't sting and make you cry. We don't want people to cry, do we? Have you ever cried? *(response)* I think we all have cried before. When you cried, did your mom or dad ever use these? **Hold up the tissues.** *(response)* What did they do with these? *(response)* Why did they wipe away your tears? *(response)* That's right, because they didn't want to see you cry, and they wanted to make you feel better.

Application: Do you know what the Bible says about heaven? It says that in heaven God will wipe away every tear from our eyes. **Hold a tissue to a child's face and gently touch it to the cheek.** Why do you think that God will wipe our tears away? *(response)* Just like our parents, he loves us and doesn't want us to feel pain. So always remember that, though sometimes on earth there is sadness, one day we will see God, and there will be no more tears, because God will wipe away every tear! Isn't that wonderful?

Let's Pray: Thank you, God, that one day we will be with you because of Jesus Christ. Thank you that you will wipe away every tear, and that you will make everything better. In Jesus' name. Amen.

Easter 5
John 13:31-35

You Shall Know They Are Mothers By Their Love

Exegetical Aim: A person's beliefs and who he/she is, is evident by one's actions. Key verses: 34-35. This may be used for Mother's Day also.

Props: A clock (big face with second hand), a stuffed animal (dog), and a photo of one of the children's moms.

Lesson: Good morning! *(response)* I have a few things to show you this morning and I want you to tell me what they are. **Hold up the clock.** What is this? *(response)* It's a clock? *(response)* How do you know it's a clock? *(it has numbers, hands)* Let's be really quiet and see if we can hear anything. What is that sound? *(ticking)* Is that what a chicken does? Does a chicken tick? *(response)* What ticks? *(response)* So you're sure this a clock? *(response)* Okay.

Hold up the dog. Now, I know what this is, this is a hippopotamus. *(no, it's a dog)* It's a dog? How do you know this is a dog? *(response)* **Their response may be descriptive of a hippo as well.** Well, a hippo has four legs, a nose, ears, and a tail and a little bit of hair. Are you sure this is a dog? *(response)* Can you make the sound of a dog? *(response)* Okay, I believe you. This is a dog!

Hold up the photo of the mom. What is this? *(photo, Mrs. _____, my mom)* A mom? Who said this was a mom? *(response)* How many of you have moms? *(response)* How do you know it's a mom? What does a mom do? *(response)* **One hopes they will say a few emotional things like love and care; if not lead them in that direction.** You know I have a mom and she hugs me. Does your mom hug you? *(response)* What does she say to you when she hugs you? *(response)* How does she show her love for you? *(response)*

Application: Do you know what a disciple is? *(no)* A disciple is a follower of Jesus. **Quickly hold up each item as you ask the following questions.** Now, how do you know this is a clock? *(response)* How do you know this is a dog? *(response)* And how do you know this is a mom? *(response)* How do you know a Christian? *(response)* Listen to this: Jesus said, "You will know they are disciples by their love for one another."

Application For Mother's Day: Do you know what today is? *(Mother's Day)* Yes, this is mom's special day. She deserves a special day because she does so much for us. And just the way a mom loves and hugs and cares for us is how we should act as followers of Jesus. Jesus said if we are his followers — his disciples — we will love and care for one another. So next time you see someone loving and caring for somebody, it could be a mom but it just might be a follower of Jesus.

Let's Pray: Lord, everyone will know we are Christians by our love for one another. Help us to love. Amen.

Easter 5
Acts 11:1-18

A Blanket Of Specialness

Exegetical Aim: To teach that God makes only special things.

Props: A sheet or a tablecloth and three other items (two very pretty items, and one very plain and worn item that has special significance to you. For instance, I will use a crystal dish, a piece of china, and an old football.) Wrap the three things in the tablecloth (sheet) and hold the tablecloth in a bundle.

Lesson: Today, I want to lay some things on the ground for you to see. But they are so special to me that I want them to remain on this sheet. Would you like to see them? *(response)* Can you guess what is inside? **Open the sheet enough for only one item to be seen.** The first item that I want you to see is this pretty crystal dish. See how it shines in the light? And I can put candy or mints in the dish. Don't you think it's pretty? *(response)* Don't you think it's special? *(response)* **Now do the same with the china. Make sure that you include the question, "Don't you think it's special?"**

I said that there are three items that I wanted to lay on the blanket to show you because they are very special to me. Why is this first dish special? *(response)* Yes, because it's pretty and shiny. And why is this piece of china special? *(response)* Right, because it is pretty, too. Now let me show you the third thing, which is very, very special. It's so special that I always take care of it, and I always know where it is. Are you ready to see it? *(response)* **Open the blanket to reveal the football.** What's the matter? Don't you think that this football is as nice as the other two things? Why not? *(response)*

You see, I got this football ten years ago just after I got married. It has a lot of scars and is worn because it has been played with so much. It has been on church trips, and family trips, and has been the cause of a lot of good memories for me. So that is why

114

this old beat up football is as special to me as these really pretty things.

Application: The Bible has a story that tells about how God showed Peter a blanket like this one with a lot of things on it, but Peter didn't think that the things on the blanket were special. But God told Peter that whatever he creates cannot be called anything but special. **Open up the sheet all the way, and have the children sit on it.** And guess what? God created you, and you are special, too. Just like this old football that doesn't look important but is because of what it means to me. We all are special to God no matter what we look like because we are his children. **Turn to the congregation.** And I want to show you all something that is very special that I have on my sheet today. **Ask the congregation to respond by saying "Amen," then turn back to the children.** You see, they think that you're special, too.

Let's Pray: Oh, God, thank you for making us. And thank you for loving us no matter who we are or what we look like. Amen.

Easter 6
John 14:23-29

Words To Remember

Exegetical Aim: To remember and obey the words of Jesus.

Props: None.

Lesson: Good morning! *(response)* I have a question. What part of our body do we use to remember things? *(response)* We all have things we need to remember. Does anyone remember their telephone number? *(response)* **Ask a few children to give their telephone numbers.** Good! Does anyone remember their address? *(response)* **Let different ones answer this time.** That's very good. Does anyone remember their parents' names? *(response)* **If possible, let the remainder respond.**

Those are all important things to remember. There are also important things we must never forget to say. What do you say when you want something? *(please)* What do you say when it's given to you? *(thank you)* What do you say when your dad tells you to do something? *(yes, sir)* **If they say "okay" respond:** You don't say, "Yeah, okay," to your dad, do you? *(response)* What do you say? *(yes, sir)* It's important to remember to say these things.

I want to play a memory game with you this morning. I'm going to divide you into two groups. **Split them down the middle.** Group one is on my left and group two is on my right. Group one, remember: Love God. Group two, remember: Love your neighbor. Okay, do you have it? Group one, what is it you're supposed to remember? *(love God)* And group two, what is it you're supposed to remember? *(love your neighbor)*

Now it gets hard. Here's a second thing to remember. Group one, remember: Seek his Kingdom. Group two, remember: Give to the poor. Okay, do you have it? Group one, what is it you're supposed to remember? *(seek his Kingdom)* And, group two, what is it you're supposed to remember? *(give to the poor)* **Now ask group one and then group two to recite the first thing and then group**

116

one then group two the second thing so that they are responding to one another.

Now it gets really hard. Here's a third thing to remember. Group one, remember: Jesus is king. Group two, remember: Humble myself. **If the children are too young, they may not know this word, so substitute "I am his child."** Okay, have you got it? Group one, what is it you're supposed to remember? *(Jesus is king)* And, group two, what is it you're supposed to remember? *(humble myself)* **Now ask group one and then group two to recite the first thing, group one then group two the second thing, and then group one then group two the third thing. Repeat all three again.**

Group #1	Group #2
Love God	Love your neighbor
Seek his Kingdom	Give to the poor
Jesus is King	Humble myself (alternative: I am his child)

Application: These are all things that Jesus asked us to remember, and Jesus tells us that if we love him we will remember and keep these words. But we forget sometimes, don't we? We forget how Jesus taught us to behave. So he did something special for us. He put his Spirit right here in our hearts to remind us of his words. The Spirit is someone who helps us remember what Jesus asks us to do. Let's all try to do these things.

Let's Pray: Let's pray by saying it again. **Ask group one and then group two to recite the first thing, then group one then group two the second thing, and then group one then group two the third thing.** Amen.

Easter 6
Acts 16:9-15

Come On In!

Exegetical Aim: To show that faithfulness leads to kindness.

Props: Three cups, two plates, and one blanket.

Lesson: Good morning! I have a story to tell you, but I can only tell it with your help. **Choose four volunteers who are generally the more behaved children. After you have chosen the volunteers, assign them their roles. One is "Traveling Christian," one is "First Person," who has one cup, one is "Second Person," who has a cup and a plate, and one is "Third Person," who has a cup, a plate, and a blanket. Stand the "Persons" in three different positions. Tell them that they must do exactly as the story tells them.**

Instruct the remainder of the children to help with sound effects. Every time someone is walking, the group should say, "Clump, clump, clump." When a person is knocking on a door, the remaining children should say, "Knock, knock, knock." When a person is preaching the good news, the children should say, "God loves you."

Let me tell you the story now. Once upon a time there was a traveling Christian, who would walk (the children should say, *clump, clump, clump*) everywhere preaching the good news (the children should say, *God loves you!*). One day he came to a house and he knocked on the door *(knock, knock, knock)*. When the first person answered the door, the Christian told her the good news *(God loves you!)*. The first person believed, and noticed that the traveling Christian had been walking *(clump, clump, clump)* a long way. The first person said that she was thankful for the good news *(God loves you!)* that God loves them and that she wanted to help the traveling Christian. So she brought the traveling Christian a drink of water. **Have "First Person" bring the cup, and "Traveling Christian" should act as though he is drinking. Retell the story using the**

118

"Second Person" in the same way, except the "Second Person" gives the "Traveling Christian" water and food, bringing a cup and a plate. **Then retell the story using the "Third Person" in the same way, except the "Third Person" invites the Christian into the home, giving food, water, and a place to sleep by laying the blanket on the floor and the Christian lying down.**

Application: Now, of the three people, who was the most grateful for hearing the good news? *(response)* Yes, you are right. The third person. One time the Apostle Paul was traveling, and a woman who heard the good news said to Paul, "If you think I have been faithful to God, please stay with us in our home." That was a very kind thing to do. If we really are happy about the good news that God loves us, and that Jesus saves us, then we will be as kind as we can to others. Let's remember that today.

Let's Pray: Thank you, God, for loving us, and for sending Jesus to save us. Help us to be kind to others because you have been kind to us. Amen.

Easter 7
John 17:20-26

Be One

Exegetical Aim: Christian Unity.

Props: Dollar sets taken out and dropped on a loud metal tray in the following order: 100 pennies, 20 nickels, 10 dimes, 4 quarters, and a dollar bill. Try to place each set in a different pocket.

Lesson: I have a dollar in my pocket and it has been rather difficult carrying it around. **Take the pennies out of your pocket and drop them slowly on the tray. Create as much sustained noise as possible. Try speaking over the noise.** They make a lot of noise and they are difficult to keep up with. Some of them actually get lost from time to time. They are a real burden to carry, too, because they are heavy.

    Remove the pennies from the tray. So I thought I would try to bring the dollar together, so I started carrying around these. **Take the nickels from your other pocket and drop them slowly on the tray.** The dollar has been a little easier to keep up with. Some of them still get lost, and they continue to make quite a bit of noise. They're still a bit of burden though.

    Remove the nickels from the tray. I thought it would be easier if the dollar could be carried around like this. **Start dropping the dimes. Drop a dime at a time.** They don't make as much noise, and I can keep up with them but occasionally I lose one. They aren't nearly as heavy though.

    Remove the dimes from the tray. Finally it occurred to me that this would be the best way to keep my dollar together. **Drop the quarters one at a time.** There's only four of them, and I rarely lose any. And even though these make a big noise, it doesn't last very long. So, do you think this is the best way to carry around a dollar? *(response)* Why not? *(you need a dollar bill)* But these four quarters are a dollar. *(a paper dollar)*

120

Application: I want you to listen to a prayer that Jesus prayed. He said, "I pray for all those who believe in me that they may be one." What did Jesus mean by that? *(response)* You're right. There are so many Christians in the world, and some of them live in America, some live in Africa, and some live in Russia. There are Methodist, Lutheran, Baptist, Catholic, and Orthodox Christians. There are so many they are hard to keep up with and they actually get lost from time to time. There are also a lot of Christians in this church of ours. Sometimes they can be difficult to deal with because they make a lot of noise and sometimes they're even a real burden.

Remove the quarters from the tray. You said I needed a dollar bill. Did you mean like this? **Drop the dollar bill on the tray.** You're right. That is a lot easier.

Let's Pray: I pray that these children will be one; that they will bring the church together; and that they will be a witness to this world. Amen.

Easter 7
Acts 16:16-34

Singing In The Chains

Exegetical Aim: To demonstrate faithfulness in the midst of strife.

Props: A chain (if possible one large enough to go around all the children), a lock, and hymn books.

Lesson: Hold up the chain. I brought a chain today because I wanted to tell you a story. How many of you would like to wear this around your hands and feet all day long and be kept from going anywhere? **Start wrapping the children in the chain while you tell the story of Paul and Silas. Use your best judgment about how to place the chain around them. The purpose is not to constrict them, just to give them an idea. Don't speak to them about what you are doing. Just tell the story. Close the lock when you have finished. Try to finish about the time you give them the hymn books.** No one wants to do that because it doesn't sound fun. As a matter of fact, if someone chained you, and then you were able to get free, what would you do? *(response)* Yes, you would try to run away. The reason I asked you that is because the Apostle Paul found himself in chains once. He and his friend Silas were put in jail because they taught about Jesus. And when they were put in jail, they had chains placed on them. Outside the jail was a guard who had to make sure that no one left. As a matter of fact, if he ever let someone go, he would be severely punished. So he kept a very close eye on the prisoners. Does that sound like a good place for Paul and Silas to be? *(response)* You're right. It wasn't a good place. If you were in a place like that, what would you want to do? *(response)* I would probably want to cry. But do you know what Paul and Silas did while they were chained? **Hand out the hymn books.** They sang hymns. Isn't that strange? They sang hymns because even in the chains they trusted God. **Ask the children to turn to a hymn they would**

know and sing one stanza with them. "Jesus Loves Me" would be appropriate.

Then do you know what happened? *(response)* There was an earthquake, and the chains around Paul and Silas came off of them, and the jail door opened. **Unlock the chain, and let the chain fall off.** So what do you think they did? *(response)* They didn't run off. They stayed right there because they didn't want the jailer to get punished. That was nice, wasn't it? And because they were so nice, the jailer believed in Jesus Christ.

Application: Paul and Silas showed what it was like to be Christian. Even though they had chains around them, they sang to God. And when they were able to run away, they chose to help someone instead. Sometimes we have very hard times that make us want to cry, but maybe in those times we should sing a song to God instead.

Let's Pray: Thank you, God, for Paul and Silas and their faith in you. Help us to sing to you even when we are sad, and even when we are in hard times, may we always remember other people who need help. In Jesus' name. Amen.

PENTECOST

Pentecost
Acts 2:1-21

Feel The Wind In Your Face

Exegetical Aim: To communicate an understanding of what happened at Pentecost.

Props: A large electric fan.

Lesson: Have the children sit tightly together. How many of you have been in a storm? *(response)* What was the first thing you felt when the storm blew in? **You want someone to say.** *(the wind)* Was anyone else with you? Did you like the wind?

What's special about the wind? *(response)* Does it feel good? *(response)* When the wind blows, does it touch just one person or does it touch everyone? *(everyone)* **Have all the children close their eyes. Have them act as though they are in prayer (hands together, heads bowed). Explain to them that they are going to feel wind, but not to open their eyes; they are to keep acting as if they are praying. Turn on the fan at its highest setting and make sure that it rotates to hit everyone or manually direct the fan to sweep across the children. While their eyes are closed, explain** Remember, don't open your eyes. Act as though you are praying. I want to tell you a story from the Bible. The disciples and some others were in a room, and they were praying. The Holy Spirit came upon them like wind. They were so excited about it that they ran outside and began to tell the other people what had happened to them. **Turn off the fan.** Now open your eyes. Did you feel the wind? *(response)* Did it feel good? *(response)* Well, just like the wind touched all of you, the Holy Spirit came upon everyone who was praying in the room with the disciples, young and old, males and females. And God promises the Holy Spirit to those who believe in him. So the Holy Spirit guides you, too, if you let the Spirit do so.

Application: Today is Pentecost. Say that with me. Pentecost. And today is the day that the Spirit came like wind to the church. You could say that today is the birthday of the church. I want you to remember the wind that touched your face and the Spirit who will be with all of you like the wind just as God promised.

Let's Pray: Almighty God, thank you for your Holy Spirit who guides and comforts us; who, like the wind, touches all of us. Amen.

Pentecost
Romans 8:14-17

Adopted Love

Exegetical Aim: Help children understand that they are part of God's family.

Props: A live puppy or kitten would be best, but a stuffed animal will do.

Lesson: I have brought something to show you today. Would you like to guess what is in this big box? *(response)* It's a puppy dog. **If it is a live puppy, explain to all of the children not to pet it yet, but just to look.** Who here has a puppy? *(response)* When you got your puppy, was it living somewhere else, and you brought it home? *(response)* That's called adopting the puppy. When people adopt a puppy, what do they do with it? How do they take care of it? *(response)* Yes, they do all kinds of things to take care of it; they give it lots of love. They keep it in a nice warm spot, and they give it something to eat and drink, and they hold it and pet it and take good care of it. Why, it even becomes a part of the family, doesn't it? It was adopted by people who loved it.

Application: Do you know what the Bible says? It says that you and I have been adopted by God! That's why we can call him Father. If God has adopted us as part of his family, what do you think God will do for us? *(response)* Yes, he will care for us, and love us, and provide for our needs. And how much more do you think God can love us than we can love a puppy? A lot more! So remember that just as we adopt a puppy dog and make it a part of the family, so God has adopted us into his family to love and care for us.

Let's Pray: Father God, thank you for adopting us into your family, and thank you for loving and caring for us always. Amen.

If you have a real animal, let the children touch it as they return to their seats. Have someone available who can take the box and the animal out of the church.

Trinity Sunday
John 16:12-15

Trinity

Exegetical Aim: To teach the Trinitarian nature of God.

Props: A solid-colored glass with ice and a clear glass with water. You want to be able to display the water but hide the ice. Optional: Hot water in a thermos or a cup on a hot plate that is hot enough to produce steam and a mirror to collect the steam.

Lesson: Hide the glass with ice and the thermos. Good morning! *(response)* I have a few things here to show to you. **Hold up the glass of water.** Can anyone tell me what I have in this glass? *(response)* What all do we do with water? *(response)* What else do we do with water? *(response)* That's right. Water is used so many ways. We grow food with it; clean things with it; we swim in it; we drink it when we're thirsty and take baths in it. What would happen if I poured this water into my hand? *(response)* Would I be able to hold the water? *(response)* I wouldn't? *(response)* Why not? *(because it is liquid or runs)* Well, let's see. **Pour just a little bit of water into your hands so that it runs to the floor through your fingers.** You're right; it does run. It's a liquid and liquids run.

   Standing up over the children with the glass of ice: Here I have another glass of water. **Hold your hands over the children's heads, ready to pour the ice into your hand as you say** I bet I can make this water stay in my hand. **The children will hurriedly move out of the way.** What? Why don't you believe me? *(response)* Watch, I will pour the whole glass of water into my hand and it won't run. **Move both hands toward the children as you pour in order to excite them. Sitting back down, show them the ice in your hand.** What is it? *(ice)* I tricked you, didn't I? *(response)* But not really. You see, this is water, but it's another form of water. It's frozen water.

   So we have two forms of water: liquid and ice. Did you know that water comes in another form? *(response)* Can anyone tell me

129

what the third form is? *(response)* **If they don't guess it:** This form doesn't run like liquid and it's not hard like ice. Sometimes you can't even see it. Does anyone know? *(response)* When water gets really hot what happens? *(steam)* Water can get so hot that it floats up into the air. You can't drink it or hold it. Most of the time you can't even see it. This kind of water is called a vapor. **Optional: At this point demonstrate the thermos and mirror or allow them to hold their hands over the thermos to feel the steam.** It's still water; it's just steamy water — like when you take a shower and the mirror gets all steamy.

Application: So water exists in three forms. What's the first? *(liquid)* What's the second? *(ice)* And what's the third? *(steam)* Three kinds of water. Today is a special day in the church. It is Trinity Sunday. We are celebrating God as Trinity. Does anyone know what Trinity means? *(response)* It means God is three persons: Father, Son, and Holy Spirit. God is like our water this morning which exists in three forms: liquid, ice, and steam. God exists in three forms: Father, Son, and Holy Spirit. We can turn that around: Liquid, ice, and steam are all what? *(water)* Water! So, Father, Son, and Holy Spirit are all who? *(God)* God. That is what the word Trinity means. God is One God but he is three persons. It's that simple! So next time you sing "Praise Father, Son, and Holy Ghost" you are celebrating the Trinity.

Let's Pray: Lord, today is Trinity Sunday, and we remember that you have revealed yourself to us as Father, Son, and Holy Spirit. Amen.

Trinity Sunday
Romans 5:1-5

Open Access

Exegetical Aim: To demonstrate that we have access to God through Christ.

Props: A key and a lock, a club membership or job identification card, and a bank card. Bring them out in a small box or bag in order to conceal them.

Lesson: Hold up the bank card. Do you know what this is? *(response)* It's my bank card. If I ever need to get some money from the bank machines, I just put this card in the slot, punch in a secret number, and I am able to get the money. That's pretty neat, huh? Now, could anybody just go to the bank and get my money? *(response)* That's right; they couldn't. How come I can get the money, but others can't? *(response)* That's right. My card gives me access to my money. **Now bring out the membership card.** Do you know what this is? **Now explain in exactly the same way that your card gives you access to your club/workplace.**

Now bring out the lock. What is this? *(response)* Right, it is a lock. Who here believes they can open it? **Let a couple of them try.** You can't do it, can you? *(response)* Is there any way that we can get into this lock? **One of them probably will guess that a key is needed. At this point, bring out the key, and select one person to come and unlock the lock.** How come she was able to unlock the lock? *(response)* Right! I gave her access by giving her the key.

Application: It's the same way with God. People just can't get to God any way they want to. But God has given us a special way that we can reach him. Does anyone know how? *(response)* By Jesus Christ. Jesus is the key. He is our access to God. In the same way I gave the key to [name of child] and she was able to open the lock, Jesus Christ has promised to bring us to the Father, who is God.

Jesus Christ is our access to God. So the next time you see a key, just remember the key God has given us: Jesus Christ.

Let's Pray: Thank you, God, for loving us so much that you would let Jesus Christ provide us with access to you. We love you. Amen.

Proper 6
Luke 7:36—8:3

You Owe Me Nothing

Exegetical Aim: Great forgiveness produces great love.

Props: Pencil over your ear, clipboard in hand, and four invoices on the clipboard. Invoices are for $1, $5, $20, and $100. To help remember this sermon, you might print it and put it on top of the clipboard.

Lesson: I have invoices here. **Take the pencil from your ear and sign the invoices as you hand them out to selected children. Once they are handed out, start with the $1 debtor:** I expect to hear something from you soon since your debt has not yet been paid. Now, you owe me $1 and I'd like to know how you are going to pay me. *(response)* Hmm? How are you going to pay me back the dollar? *(response)*

   Next Child: How about you? **Look at your clipboard to check your totals.** Your total bill comes to $5. When do you think that you'll be able to get that to me? *(response)*

   And you! You know **look at the clip board to check total** you owe me $20. Have you got that kind of cash? *(response)* We do accept MasterCard, Visa, Diners, American Express, and Discover. You can even use our e-commerce account at www.youowememoney.com. So, do you want to pay by credit card or check? *(response)* **Impatiently bang your pencil on the front edge of your clip board.**

   Address the fourth debtor. I don't even know what to do with you! Did you know that your bill is now $100? You owe me $100! And on top of that, interest is accruing on this debt. How and when are you going to pay? *(response)* This is no laughing matter, young man. This is a lot of money. *(response)*

   What am I going to do with you dead beats? **Pause and look at the debtors.** Tell you what. I'm going to forgive all these debts. **Take the invoices one at a time and mark on each of them "Paid**

133

In Full." You might use a red pen or purchase some stickers that say this. As you hand each of them their cancelled debts, say the following: You no longer owe me $1. Your $5 debt is cancelled. Your $20, consider it paid. For you, who owes $100, it is forgiven.

Now let me ask all of you. Which of these four will love me more? *(the one who owed the $100)*

Application: So it is with God. Who do you think is going to love God more? The person who has been forgiven a little mistake or the person who has been forgiven a big mistake? *(response)* When you make a little mistake and he forgives you, you appreciate it, don't you? *(response)* But, when you have done something terrible and sinful and very bad and he forgives you, then how much do you love God? *(response)*

Let's Pray: Father, we are grateful that you overlook our little sins, but we love you because you forgive us when we make terrible mistakes. Amen.

Proper 6
Galatians 2:15-21

To Rebuild Or Not To Rebuild

Exegetical Aim: To explain that we should not keep doing things that we know are wrong.

Props: Some building blocks.

Lesson: As you talk to the children, illustrate by using the building blocks. Begin by building a "barn" with a couple of blocks falling off, and then adapt the structure as you tell the story. Sometimes you can drive on the highway or out in the country and see an old barn that is falling in. Have any of you ever seen an old barn that was falling in and rotting? *(response)* When a barn gets to be like that, can the horses and chickens stay inside of it to keep dry and warm? *(response)* No, they can't, because it is a dangerous place, right? When barns get to be in really bad shape, what do you think the farmer eventually does? *(response)* Yes, he tears it down in order to build a new one. If a farmer is going to build a new barn, should he get new boards, or should he use the really bad ones that he just tore down? *(response)* That's right, he should use new boards and make it a strong barn. What would you say to the farmer if he tore down the barn, and then used the old wood to build it back? *(response)* Yes, you would say that the farmer would not be very smart.

Application: Did you know that Saint Paul talked about this? He said that it is not smart to build back the same thing that you tear down. He meant that if we are acting in a way that is bad, we should begin to act a new way. But if we say we are sorry for acting a certain way and then go back and do it again, we are doing the same thing as the farmer who built the old barn back after he tore it down. We are not being smart if we keep doing the same bad things over and over, are we? *(response)* Saint Paul reminds us that when we turn to Jesus, then we are no longer building up what we tore down. So this week, let us remember not to keep doing bad things over and over again. And the next time you see some blocks, you will remember not to build up the same things that you've torn down.

Let's Pray: Dear God, help us not to do bad things over and over. Let us turn to Jesus so that we don't build up what we've torn down. In Jesus' name. Amen.

✝

Proper 7
Luke 8:26-39

Big Rocks

Exegetical Aim: We must fill our lives with the important things first or the smaller things will overtake us.

Props: One-gallon wide-mouthed mason jar (a pickle jar would be great), a dozen fist-sized rocks, a container of gravel, a container of sand, and a container of water. I suggest you try the illustration once before doing it in front of the children. You must hide the various elements to make this illustration effective.

Lesson: Okay, time for a quiz. **Put the one-gallon, wide-mouthed mason jar in the middle of them. Carefully place the dozen fist-sized rocks, one at a time, into the jar.**
    When the jar is full and no more rocks will fit inside: Is this jar full? *(yes)* Really? **As you dump in the gravel, shake the jar causing the pieces of gravel to work themselves down into the spaces between the big rocks.**
    There we go! Is the jar full? *(response)* **If some say, "No,"** say, Good! **If all say, "Yes," say, Really? Bring out the container of sand. Pour the sand in between the cracks; fill the jar so that all the spaces left between the rocks and the gravel are filled. Some shaking may be required. Ask the question once more,** Is this jar full? *(no)* **You hope they are onto you now and will answer negatively** Good! **With the pitcher of water, fill the jar to the brim.** Now is it full? *(no)* Yes, it is! It is now full. What is the point of this illustration? *(response)* **Give them time and several attempts at the answer.**
    Here is the actual point of the illustration: What this teaches us is: If you don't put the big rocks in first, you'll never get them in at all.

Application: What are the big rocks in your life? *(response)* Here is a big rock: Spending time praying and reading the Bible. Can you think of another? *(response)* Here is another big rock: Spending time with your brother or sister or your mom or dad or your grandparents. Or reading a book. Can you think of any other big rocks? *(response)* Maybe doing something at church. Teaching others. Doing your homework. Remember to put the BIG ROCKS in first or you'll never get them in at all.

So, tonight when you are saying your prayers, think about what we did this morning, and ask yourself this question: What are the "big rocks" in my life? Then, put those in your jar.

Let's Pray: Lord, we want to be sure to do the most important things first, to put the big rocks in before we put the sand in. Help us to do just that. Amen.

If you are using this on Father's Day, you can talk about how fathers make their children their first priority.

Proper 7
Galatians 3:23-29

Belonging To Christ

Exegetical Aim: To show that once we belong to Christ, there is no distinction among us.

Props: Some sort of strong bag or carrier (duffel bag, athletic bag, and so forth), and a football, a basketball, and a soccer ball.

Lesson: Today I brought my bag to show you. This is my bag, and the things inside are mine. There are some different things inside, but they are all mine because they are in my bag. Would you like to see what is inside? *(response)* As I bring them out, you tell me what they are, okay? *(response)* Here goes. What is this? *(football)* How did you know it was a football? *(response)* Oh, because of the way it was shaped, and because of the lacing, and because it is brown. I see. Okay, here's the next one. What is this? *(basketball)* How did you know it was a basketball? **Follow the same pattern for the soccer ball.** Now I'm going to put these back in my bag and zip it up. Now, whose bag is this? *(yours)* That's right; it is my bag. So the things inside belong to whom? *(you)* Right. Even though the things are different, it doesn't matter what they look like once they are in my bag. They belong to me, and people know not to take them.

Application: I have one more question. Whose are you? *(response)* Saint Paul said that you and I belong to Christ. And because you and I belong to Christ, it doesn't matter if we are a boy or a girl, or an American, an Asian, an African, or a European. If we belong to Christ, all that matters is that we are his, and he will not let anyone take us. No matter where we go in life, and no matter what happens, we belong to Christ. So just like this bag and its contents are mine, to whom do you belong? *(Christ)*

Let's Pray: Thank you, Father, that we belong to Christ, and that no one can take us. Amen.

Proper 8
Luke 9:51-62

Finish What You Started

Exegetical Aim: Jesus has "set his face to Jerusalem" and is determined to fulfill the will of God. The Disciples are asked to put their hand to the plow and not look back, i.e., to finish what has been started.

Props: An ability to sing the ABC song.

Lesson: I need your help this morning. Would you teach me the ABC song? *(response)* For some reason I just can't seem to learn it. How does it start? *(response)* **When they start it, join in and when you get to "G" make it the interjection not the letter of the alphabet. The idea is to interrupt the song. Make the "Gee" loud:** ABCDEF Gee, I've got a really bad itch. **Reach down to scratch your leg.** Boy, that feels good. **Stop scratching, sigh, and pause.** Ahhh...Oh! I'm sorry what were we doing? *(response)* Oh yeah, you were teaching me the alphabet song. **Let them start again** How does it go? *(abcdef ...)* ABCDEFGH I, I, I, I am so hungry! Are you hungry? You know what I'd like? I'd like a peanut butter and jelly sandwich. Yeah, that would be really good right about now. **Pause as if you're thinking about the sandwich and mumble:** Peanut butter and jelly ... What? *(response)* What's wrong? *(response)* The ABC's? You were teaching me the ABC's. Okay, go ahead and teach me. *(abcdef ...)* ABCDEFGHIJKLMN Oh, Oh, Oh yeah, and a big glass of chocolate milk! Wouldn't that be great? A big glass of chocolate milk, cold. It would have to be really cold and a peanut butter and jelly sandwich. That's what I want. **Pause** *(response)* What is it? *(response)* The ABC's?

Oh, I'm never going to learn the ABC song. Can you tell me why I can't learn the ABC's? *(you've got to finish the song)* I've got to do what? *(finish the song)* **You hope they will give this answer. If not, then ask, "How can I make it all the way to**

XYZ?" You mean if I sing the song all the way through I will learn my ABCs? *(response)*

Application: I remember Jesus saying something like that. He said, "Put your hand to the plow and don't look back." Does anyone know what a plow is? *(response)* A plow is something a farmer uses to plant seeds. The plow turns up the ground and makes straight lines in the dirt. Horses and cows are used to pull the plows, but now machines and tractors do all that work. Have you ever noticed how a farmer's field has straight lines in the dirt? *(response)* Do you know how they make all those straight lines? The farmer keeps his eyes on some object in front of him. He looks ahead to the other side of the field. **Point to some object in the sanctuary.** He picks a tree or a light post and he heads straight for it. He never looks back. If he looks back, the plow might get crooked, and if the plow gets crooked, what happens? *(the lines get crooked)* Jesus told his disciples to keep their eyes on him and not to look back.

When mom or dad ask you to pick up your toys or help out around the house, you can't be distracted. You can't look around for other things to do. We have to start our job and finish the job we started. Now, I'm going to finish what I started. Teach me the whole song this time: ABCDEF ... Now I know my ABCs next time won't you sing with me. Now I know my ABC's because I finished what I started.

Let's Pray: Lord, I will finish what I start. Amen.

Proper 8
Galatians 5:1, 13-25

There Is No Law Against Such Things

Exegetical Aim: For some things there are no laws.

Props: Actual signs or pictures of signs that forbid things; i.e., No Smoking, STOP, No Talking, etc. Also, make a sign saying, "No Smiling," with a picture of a smile and an X through it.

Lesson: Today I want to talk to you about rules. I want you to tell me what rule each sign is talking about. Let's try one. **Hold up the STOP sign.** What does this sign mean? *(response)* Where do you see this sign? *(response)* **Now do the same with the other signs. At the very last, bring out the No Smiling sign.** Have you ever seen this sign? *(response)* Do you know what kind of sign this is? *(response)* This is a No Smiling sign. Is that a strange sort of sign to have? *(response)* Why? *(response)* You're right; there's nothing wrong with smiling. What are other things that there's nothing wrong with? *(response)* Is there anything wrong with loving someone, or helping someone, or being thoughtful? *(response)* Why? *(response)*

Application: That's exactly what the Apostle Paul said to one of the early churches. He said there's not a sign or a rule that says you can't be nice. And since we are disciples of Jesus, we have to live a life of love and care, because it doesn't break any rules. So let us do two things this week: every day love and care for everyone. There's not a single rule or a sign that says you can't do that! And it is what Jesus would want us to do.

Let's Pray: Dear Father, give us the strength to care for and love others, because there is not a law keeping us from doing that. In Jesus' name. Amen.

Proper 9
Luke 10:1-11, 16-20

Written In The Heavens

Exegetical Aim: The Kingdom of God surrounds us (v. 9) and our names are written in heaven (v. 20).

Props: An XXL white t-shirt and permanent markers. Hide the t-shirt.

Lesson: I have a question for you this morning: Name something that we are all very close to all day long. *(ground)* Even closer than the ground. *(home, trees, parents are possible answers)* Those are all good answers, but they're not what I am thinking of. All day long we are closer to this than we are to anything else. Can you guess what it is? *(response)* It is so close to us, it touches our skin. *(clothes)* **When they give the right answer bring out the t-shirt.** What do I have with me this morning? *(response)* They are very close to us. They cover our shoulders, our chest, and our stomachs.

I also brought some markers this morning and we're going to write our names on this t-shirt. **Do this now and have the older ones help the younger ones or assist them yourself.**

Application: Hold up the t-shirt. Jesus said something that reminds me of this t-shirt. He said, "The Kingdom of God is near you." Can you imagine that? Heaven itself is near us. **Hold the shirt to your torso or put it on.** Just like a t-shirt, it surrounds us, warms us, covers our hearts, and protects us. Jesus said something else that reminds me of this t-shirt. He said, "Be happy (rejoice) because your names are written in heaven." Not only is heaven near you but God is so close to you that he knows your name and he has written your name down in heaven. How wonderful it is to know that heaven surrounds us and that God knows us by name.

Let's Pray: Lord, I pray that these children learn that your kingdom is closer to them than anything else in the world, even closer than a t-shirt. Amen.

Proper 9
Galatians 6:(1-6) 7-16

Beginnings And Endings

Exegetical Aim: Whatever a man sows, so shall he reap.

Props: An egg, a picture of an elephant, a handful of Cheerios, a doughnut, a flower seed, and a potted flower.

Lesson: Today I thought that I would show you some beginnings and some endings. I'll show you something that's a beginning, and then I'll show you what I think the ending will be. Okay? **Hold up the egg.** For instance, if I hold up this egg and say this is the beginning, then I know what the end will be, right? **Hold up the picture of the elephant.** *(no)* What do you mean, "No!" Won't an elephant come out of an egg like this? *(response)* Oh, I see. A chicken will come from an egg. Well, let's try another one. **Hold up the Cheerios.** Now if this is the beginning, and I plant this in the ground, what would be the end? **Let them guess for a moment, then hold up the doughnut.** If you plant Cheerios in the ground, won't they become doughnuts? *(no)* Oh, dear, I'm really messing up, aren't I? Let me try one more.

Hold up the little flower seeds. If I plant these flower seeds, what would I get? Would I get this? **Hold up the potted plant.** *(yes)* Oh good, I got one right! Now how do you know that if I plant this seed a flower will come? *(response)* That's right, this is a flower seed. What will become of the egg? *(a chicken)* And what will become of the Cheerios? *(a bowl of cereal)*

Application: The Bible says whatever you plant will be the thing that grows. If you are mean to someone, how will they be to you? *(response)* That's right. They will be mean to you. If you plant mean words, and name calling, it will only turn out bad for everyone. But if you plant niceness in people, and love them, and treat them like you want to be treated, then they will treat you well, and

146

it will work out for the best. Remember, whatever you plant will be the thing that grows.

Let's Pray: Gracious Father, thank you for the seeds that grow into flowers. They remind us to plant good things in our lives so that your goodness can grow. In Jesus' name we pray. Amen.

Proper 10
Luke 10:25-37

Who's My Friend?

Exegetical Aim: We should not discriminately pick who we love, so we must love all.

Props: A pair of glasses, a book or pamphlet in a foreign language, and a prescription bottle.

Lesson: Good morning! *(response)* There is a wonderful story in the Bible about a boy who was walking down the street and some bullies surprised him and beat him up and took his milk money away from him. And then they just left him in the street. Then a friend of his, a neighbor, was walking down the road and saw the boy all beaten up, but he passed him right by because there was this show on television and it was about to start and he didn't want to miss it.

Then, what do you know, another friend, a girl who lived down the street, was riding her bike down that road and when she saw the boy all beaten up she thought to herself, "Well, that's a shame. That poor boy is in trouble." She thought about it and she said to herself, "I would stop and help but I don't have enough room on my bike to carry him." And she passed him by.

Then a Mexican boy who spoke Spanish came along, and he only knew a little bit of English. **(You may choose to use a black boy as an example or a white boy depending on the context of your congregation.)** He didn't live in the neighborhood and didn't even know the boy who was hurt. When he saw the boy, he stopped and asked if he was okay and helped the boy up and carried him home.

Now, here is my question for you: Which one of these was a friend to the boy who was hurt? *(the Mexican boy)*

Application: We are all very different. **Hold up the glasses.** What do I have in my hand? *(response)* That's right. Some people wear glasses to help them see. **If there are children with glasses on, you may ask them how important the glasses are to them. Hold up the book.** Can anyone read this for me? **Hand it to one of the older children.** Can you read that? *(no)* That's because it's not English; it's in Spanish. Not everyone speaks English like we do. They come from a different country and they live differently than we do. Some children even look different. Some are red, some are yellow, some are black and some are white. **Hold up the prescription bottle.** And then there are children who get sick, and they have to take medicine or they may have to live in a wheelchair. We are all very different.

The differences don't matter, do they? *(response)* You might have freckles or you might be black. You might wear glasses or have red hair. Either way, you are still my friend, and if you are ever in trouble I want to help you.

Let's Pray: Lord, teach us to be a friend to those who are different and especially to those who are in desperate need of help. Amen.

Proper 10
Colossians 1:1-14

Thanksgiving And Prayer

Exegetical Aim: God brings light through his Son.

Props: A flashlight, a large bag that would be dark inside (example: a thick black garbage bag), eyeglasses, binoculars or magnifying glass, and a cross to fit in the bag.

Lesson: Today I brought a very big bag and something is at the bottom of it, but I am not sure what it is. Can you tell me what it is? *(response)* What? You don't know? *(response)* Someone will have to look inside and see what it is. **Choose a volunteer, and slightly open the bag so that it remains too dark to see.** Now can you tell me what is inside of the bag? *(response)* No? Well, maybe we need some help. **Get another volunteer and hand him/her eyeglasses.** Put these on and look inside. Can you tell me what is in the bottom of the bag? *(response)* The glasses didn't work, did they? Let's try something else. **Use another volunteer and give him/her binoculars or a magnifying glass.** Look through this and tell me what's at the bottom. Can you see? *(response)* I wonder why we haven't been able to see the object? *(response)* Oh, it's too dark!

We need a way to see in the dark, don't we. What could we use? *(a light or a flashlight)* Funny you should say that. Look what I have — a flashlight! **Get another volunteer to look inside using the flashlight.** What is it? Tell us; what's in the bag? *(response)* A cross? **Optional: If you have a small number of children, give everyone a chance to look into the bag.** Let me check and see if there really is a cross down in the bottom. **Pull out the cross.** It is a cross!

Application: The Apostle Paul told us that as Christians we are children of the light. We should be good and remind people of things that are good. We should use our light — the lives we've been given — to shine on the cross. What are some ways that we can shine our light? *(response)* So remember that you are children of the ... *(light)*, and you are to remind everyone that Jesus died for them on the ... *(cross)*.

Let's Pray: Dear God, thank you that your Son Jesus Christ died on the cross for our sins. Let us live so as to show your light to the world. In Jesus' name we pray. Amen.

Proper 11
Luke 10:38-42

Work And Worship

Exegetical Aim: Sometimes we need to sit still, listen, and worship and not let the cares of this world draw us away from God.

Props: A pot and a ladle. All other props are imaginary.

Lesson: As the children sit down, you look busy and distracted stirring and cooking. Oh, I am so glad I came to church this morning! **Motion to a place behind one of the children.** Hand me some of that garlic over there. *(response)* **The children will likely play along with you. If not motion again:** Some of that garlic right there behind you. Hurry it up now! *(response)* As I was saying, it's good to be in church this morning because I do enjoy cooking and making all this delicious food for you to eat. **Taste the food from the ladle.** Hmm? Needs a little pepper. **Point behind some of the other children.** Hand me that pepper there. *(response)* **Shaking in the spices:** You know, that's why we come to church — to prepare food and cook and clean and get all our work done. *(response, if any)* Now, all done! **Act as though you are serving the food.** Hold out your bowls. Well, hold them out. Here's your food. **Put down the pot and ladle and act as though you are eating.** Do you like it? Yes, I sure am busy today here at church with all this work and cooking and all. When I am done eating I have to sweep and mop and vacuum, don't I? *(response)* What? *(response)* Isn't that what I am supposed to do on Sunday morning in church? *(no)* It's not? What am I supposed to do? *(response)* **You may want to continue questioning them.** What else can I do in church? *(response)* You mean I don't have to work all the time? *(response)* When I come to church I can stop **hold up the pot and ladle** all this? I can be still and think about God and how much he loves me? *(response)*

Application: There is a word for what you're talking about. Do you know what that word is? *(response)* We call it "worship." We worship God in church, don't we? *(response)* Worship is very important in our lives. It is a time for me to leave all my chores at home and come to God with empty hands. **Hold out your hands to the children — palms up.** No hammer in my hand. No broom. No brief case. No pots and pans. No cell phone. Nothing. Just hands that are empty and anxious to hold God's hand.

Let's Pray: Lord, I put down my chores and come to you this morning with empty hands. Amen.

Proper 11
Colossians 1:15-28

Christ Is The Head

Exegetical Aim: To explain that Christ is the head of the church.

Props: A Mr. Potato Head toy.

Lesson: Today I want to show you a toy that I used to play with when I was a child. Would you like to see it? *(response)* Okay, let me show you. **Bring out the Mr. Potato Head without anything on it.** Have you ever played with this? *(response)* Can you help me remember how to play with it? What do I need to add to the head? **Spend time placing ears, eyes, mouth, and hat on the head. Let the children guide you.** Wow, that's looking pretty good, isn't it? When you play with Mr. Potato Head, do you ever change the pieces around and make funny faces? *(response)* Let's do that. **Now place the ear where the mouth goes, etc., until it looks silly. Again, let the children guide you.** What does he look like now? *(response)* Even though it looks different, there is still one thing that is the same as the last one we made. Who can guess what is the same? **Guide the children into saying that the head is the same.** You are right. The head is the same. Tell me, could we make faces without the head? *(response)* No, we couldn't. Because without the head, there isn't a Mr. Potato Head. Without the head, there isn't a game to play.

Application: Did you know that it is the same with the church. There are many different churches, and many of them look different and have different looking people, but there is one thing that is the same. Do you know what it is? *(responses, if any)* They all believe in Jesus Christ as the Savior. Saint Paul said that Christ is the head of the church. Say that with me. Christ *(Christ)* is the head *(is the head)* of the church *(of the church)*. By that he meant that without Jesus there is no church. As much as we try to have church or be the church, if we do not have Jesus, there is no church.

Just like there is no game to play without the head, there is no church without Jesus. So the next time you play with your Mr. Potato Head, I want you to remember what Saint Paul said about Jesus. Say it with me one more time. Christ *(Christ)* is the head *(is the head)* of the church *(of the church)*.

Let's Pray: Dear God, thank you that your Son Jesus Christ is the head of the church. Help us always to remember that we cannot be a church without him. Amen.

Proper 12
Luke 11:1-13

Magic Prayers

Exegetical Aim: To teach the children that prayer forms a relationship with God.

Props: An empty wallet or purse.

Lesson: Good morning. *(response)* **Holding up the wallet/purse, thumb through it and show that it is empty.** I want you to look at this! There's nothing in here. I need to do something about this empty wallet. Let's see ... what can I do about this? **Show that you are thinking by tapping on your temple. If there is a response from the children ignore it.** I know ... I gotta pray about this. There are a few things I've wanted to talk to God about, and I can pray about this too ... Let's pray.

    Casually you begin to pray: God, I want a lot of money. You see, there's this red jeep. It's really nice and I think I'd look really good in it driving around town. And, I'd like some really big muscles. You made me kind of puny and if, well, if you could change that I'd be very happy. Oh, and one last thing. I've noticed something very strange about my hair. There's not as much of it as there once was and it's turning a strange color. I know it sounds strange, but it actually looks as if it's turning gray. So if you could stop that. Amen.

    Well, that ought to about do it! **Hold up the wallet and check to see if the money has magically appeared. Continue to look through the wallet and say to yourself:** What happened? *(response)* There's no money in here. **Now address the children.** What happened? Why didn't I get any money? *(response)* **Your guess is as good as mine as to what the children will answer — be on your toes.** And I don't feel any stronger. **Feel your arm.** Why didn't God give me bigger muscles? *(response)* Does my hair look any better? *(response)* Why is that? *(response)*

Application: Affirm one of the correct responses: That's right. You know that I'm teasing you, don't you? *(response)* We really can't pray like that and expect God to answer. What kind of things should we pray for? *(response)* **Give them time to answer. In addition to the children's answers:** We can pray for God's will to be done in our lives. We can pray for our food. We can pray that God will help us to forgive one another and to help us do what is right and good. That's what real prayer is: we put away our selfish thoughts and we pray that God will help us love one another. That's how Jesus taught us to pray.

Let's Pray: Pray the Lord's Prayer or do this children's version. I'll pray the right way this time: Father in heaven, we ask for your will to be done in our lives. Please bless us with food today and forgive us when we sin. We forgive those who have hurt us. Help us above all to be good. Amen!

Proper 12
Colossians 2:6-15 (16-19)

Nailed Forgiveness

Exegetical Aim: To show that forgiveness came to us on the cross.

Props: A small cross, a hammer, nails, and paper.

Lesson: Hold up the cross. I believe all of you know what I have in my hand. *(response)* Yes, it's a cross. Tell me why it's important to us. *(response)* Yes, that's right; Jesus died on the cross. But do you know that God made something good come out of it? When Jesus died, our sins were forgiven. Can someone tell me what sins are? *(response)* Can you name any sins? *(response)* **Write down the answers on individual pieces of paper. Do no more than four.** Yes, all of these things are sins. And in our lives we do these things. Sometimes we do them on purpose, other times by accident, but we always need to ask for forgiveness. And when we do ask for forgiveness, the Bible promises that something wonderful will happen.

Application: Take out the hammer and nails from where they were hidden. Take one of the pieces of paper, and prepare to nail it on the cross. The Apostle Paul said that when Jesus died **begin to nail the first piece of paper,** he took our sins, **nail the next piece of paper,** and all the things against us, **nail the next piece,** and nailed them to his cross, **nail the last piece. Hold up the cross.** Your sins and my sins are nailed to the cross because Jesus loves us. The next time you see a cross, you can remember that Jesus nailed our sins to it. Be thankful that our sins have been forgiven.

Let's Pray: Dear God, thank you for Jesus Christ and how our sins have been nailed to the cross. When we see the cross, we know that on that cross Jesus forgave our sins. Amen.

Proper 13
Luke 12:13-21

Gobble, Gobble, Gone

Exegetical Aim: A lesson of sharing.

Props: M&M's. You will need: 1) A small package for you to eat. If you cannot eat the whole bag in a single sitting, then slightly open the bag, empty the bag, and place what you can't eat back in. But it needs to be proportioned to the number of children so that it looks as though you could have shared. If you are preaching afterwards, you'll need some water at the pulpit to wash them down. 2) One package for each child present. Hide these packages.

Lesson: Good morning! *(response)* **Hold up a single package of M&M's:** I have a package of my favorite candy with me this morning. What are they? *(response)* Who likes M&M's? *(response)* **Tear open the bag while talking to the children.** You do? I do too! **Pour the M&M's into your hands and start picking out the greens.** My favorite M&M's are the green ones. **Hold out all the greens.** Look at all those green M&M's. Don't they look great? *(response)* **Now eat them. Take a little time to chew and enjoy and nod to the children in approval. Leave your hand open so they see the others.**

Boy, that was good. I sure do like the green ones ... **look down at the M&M's and pick out the brown,** but, you know, these brown ones remind me of chocolate and I love chocolate. **Put all the brown in your mouth. With a full mouth and holding the candies in front, say,** What's your favorite color? *(red)* Really? **Point to red.** You like the red? **Start picking them out.** They do look good! **Put them all in your mouth.** Yeah, **crunch,** yeah, **crunch,** you're right, **crunch,** they are good.

Do you like this color? *(response)* How about this one? *(response)* I bet they're good, too. **Put them all in your mouth.** Mmm! **crunch** They are good. **Crunch, crunch. Start to register some concern on your face. Looking at the children with your mouth**

still a bit full: What? **Slowly crunch.** What's wrong? *(you ate them all; you didn't share)*. I should have shared? *(response)* Gosh, that wasn't very nice of me, was it? *(response)* I didn't think of you at all. I was only thinking about myself.

Application: Jesus told a story about a man like that. He grew a whole lot of corn and wheat on his farm. Then he built a big barn and he put it all in the barn for himself, and he didn't share it with anyone. Do you know what happened to that man? *(response)* On the very day he put all that food in the barn, he died. He thought he'd be able to gobble all that food by himself. Next thing you know he's gone. He never ate the food and he missed an opportunity to share it with others.

We need to do what Jesus told us to do. We need to share. **Pull out the other M&M's and share with the children.** Take these back with you and give them to your parents. You may eat them after church!

Let's Pray: Father, teach us to share with one another not just small things like M&M's but big things as well. Amen.

Proper 13
Colossians 3:1-11

All In All

Exegetical Aim: To demonstrate that there is no partiality in Christ. Key verse: 11.

Props: A bowl of plain M&M's.

Lesson: Today I want to share with you some of my favorite candy. **Show them the candy.** What kind is it? *(M&M's)* Right! M&M's! Let's all say, yea! *(response)* I'm going to give each of you some of this, but first you have to tell me which color you like the best. *(response)* I personally like the brown ones. Who likes green? *(response)* Red? *(response)* Orange? *(response)* The new blue? *(response)* Well, here's what I want you to do. Each of you can get three. But when you get them, close your eyes or turn your head away and reach into the bowl and don't look at them. Keep them closed in your hand. Okay, come and get them, and remember, don't look at them. **When everyone has their M&M's:** Now on the count of three, without looking at your M&M's, open your mouth, and eat them. 1, 2, 3! **Make sure everyone follows the instructions. After the children have eaten:** What colors did you eat? Who ate a red one? *(response)* Who ate a green? *(response)* **Keep asking until someone says, "We don't know," or "They all taste the same."**

Application: That's right. Inside the different shells they all taste the same. Did you know that in a way Christians are like those M&M's? That's what the Apostle Paul said. He said that when Christ is in you and you are in Christ, there are no differences between us. We're neither black nor white, rich nor poor, or even male nor female. It doesn't make a difference to God what kind of shell we have — the inside is what counts to him. And it shouldn't matter to us either. We should treat everyone the same no matter what color their shell.

161

Let's Pray: Dear God, thank you for loving us no matter the color of our shell, and thank you for Jesus Christ, who makes us all children of God. Amen.

Proper 14
Luke 12:32-40

Watch And Be Ready!

Exegetical Aim: Conditioning God's children to be watchful and ready.

Props: A tennis ball or something comparable.

Lesson: Tossing the ball from hand to hand: Good morning! *(response)* A long, long time ago, when people used candles and lamps to see at night because there was no electricity, there was this man and he left home to go to a party. His maids and his servants had no idea when he would return home, so they waited into the night for him to come home. **Toss the ball from the waist to one of the children. Don't telecast your toss; make it immediate so it is a surprise. Motion for the ball to be returned to you — do not ask for it.** It was getting late and the man had not returned home. The maids and the servants kept looking out the windows and wondering when their master would return. **Toss the ball from the waist to another child. Motion for the ball to be returned.**

Now it was very late, all the stars were out and the moon was slowly sinking down. All the maids and servants who were waiting for their master to return from the party were very tired and sleepy. What do you think they did? *(response)* **Toss the ball from the waist to another child. Motion for the ball to be returned.** Well, they kept the lamps and candles burning all night, and they stayed up because when the master came home they wanted to meet him at the door, welcome him home, and help him get ready for bed. **Toss the ball once more from the waist. Motion for the ball to be returned. It doesn't matter if the ball is caught by a child — it is enough that they are watching for you to throw it.**

Application: At first you were surprised when I threw the ball at you and you weren't able to catch it. But then what happened? *(we*

163

caught it) Yes, you learned to be ready. You were watching for me to toss it to you. **If no one caught the ball, then simply explain that they at least were watching for you to throw it. Now, hold up the ball:** This is what we are doing as Christians. We are watching for Jesus to come back. He is going to come back one day and it might be soon. **Fake a throw to one of the children.** And we need to be ready.

How can we get ourselves ready for his coming? *(response)* We can love God and love one another. How do we help people who are hungry? *(response)* How can we help people who need clothes? *(response)* If someone is sick, what can we do for them? *(response)* That's right. What else can we do? *(pray, read our Bibles, etc.)* These are ways that we can be good maids and servants waiting for our master to come. **Toss the ball high in the air into the middle of the children or throw it straight up so that you catch it. Let's not be surprised when Jesus returns. Let's be watching and ready!**

Let's Pray: Lord, help your children to be ready when you return. Amen.

Proper 14
Hebrews 11:1-3, 8-16

Faith

Exegetical Aim: Faith is the substance of things hoped for.

Props: Someone to work the lights of the church. You must talk to this person beforehand, and have him/her prepared to time his/her task perfectly.

Lesson: Good morning. Today I want to tell you that something different is going to happen in church today. Something really different. Do you believe me? *(response)* As a matter of fact, something really different is going to happen while you are sitting here. Do you believe me? *(response)* You really have to believe me. Okay. This is what's going to happen. The lights are going to go out! That's right; the lights out — poof! In church! Cool, huh? **You might determine beforehand if you want all the lights or just some of the lights. Obviously, the more lights that go out, the more effective the demonstration.** Do you want this to happen? *(response)* Okay. But there's only one way for the lights to go off. I need someone to walk by himself/herself over to the wall, and knock three times. If you do that, the lights will go out. Do you believe me? **Send a volunteer to knock on the wall. The person working the lights will immediately turn the designated lights off after the third knock, and then back on after a couple of seconds.**

Application: Did you think that was really going to work? Usually, you have to turn on a light switch to make lights turn on and off. But I knew it would work if you knocked. Do you know how I knew? Because before you got here, I talked to [name of the light person] and instructed him/her to turn the lights off at just the right moment. Even though you didn't know how it was going to happen, I knew. You trusted in me that it would happen. That's called faith. You had faith in my words.

There was a man named Abraham who believed God's word. God promised him something strange. God said, Abraham, you're an old man, but you and your wife are going to have a child and you will become the father of many nations. Abraham believed God even though God's promise sounded strange. Then it happened. They actually had a baby and they named him Isaac. Abraham trusted in God. He had faith.

We are called to have the same faith in God's word even when we don't fully understand. We have to trust that God knows what he is doing. Study your Bibles, because in it you will find God's promises and you can trust in those promises. We call that having faith.

Let's Pray: Dear God, we trust in you even when it seems strange to do so. Amen.

Proper 15
Luke 12:49-56

Sign Of The Times

Exegetical Aim: Winter and cold as symbols and signs of the world's darkness and the need for God's intervention. (This Children's Sermon is a bit more symbolic than usual, but so is the scriptural text.)

Props: A branch with enough green leaves for each child to tear one off.

Lesson: As you were coming to church this morning perhaps you noticed the weather. What was the weather like? *(response)* What kind of things did you see? What kind of sky was there? *(response)* What was the temperature like? Was it hot, cold, or nice outside? *(response)* **Summarize the weather conditions and then add to the end of your description:** But weather can change quickly, can't it? *(response)* How do you know when it's going to rain? *(response)* That is right. It can be sunny outside, the sky nice and blue, and the sun shining brightly, and then you see some dark clouds coming, and you hear the thunder in the distance, and that means it's going to rain.

    Hold up the branch. What do I have this morning? *(response)* What color are the leaves? *(response)* They are green because it's still summer. What is going to happen to the leaves in a few weeks? *(response)* **If they don't know:** Are the leaves going to change? *(response)* What colors? *(response)* All those colors are a sign that something is on the way. What is on the way? How is the weather going to change? *(cold, winter)* And when it gets cold what happens? *(response)* It snows. **Hold up the branch.** And how do we know that winter is on the way? *(response)*

Application: I want everyone to come up and take a leaf. Take one leaf. Take them off at the branch slowly so you don't tear the leaves. Okay, sit back down. **When they are seated:** Take a look at your

leaf. Soon millions and millions of leaves like the one you're holding will change color, turn brown, die, and fall to the ground. And
then the cold will come. And when it gets cold in the world we
need God very much to warm our hearts and make us feel love
again. You see, the cold not only kills the leaves, but it deadens our
hearts, and God wants very much to come into our hearts and warm
them with his love so they don't die and fall to the ground.

Let's Pray: Lord, keep our hearts warm. Keep us from being cold-
hearted. Amen.

Proper 15
Hebrews 11:29—12:2

They Are Cheering You On!

Exegetical Aim: Explanation of the concept: a great cloud of witnesses.

Props: A basketball, ballet shoes, a tennis ball, and some running shoes concealed in a container of some sort.

Lesson: I've got some things here today that I want to show you. Are you ready? **First hold up the basketball for just a brief moment, then hide it again.** Did you see my football? *(response)* What was it then? *(response)* A basketball? Okay, you were right. **Bring out the basketball.** Who likes playing basketball? *(response)* **Repeat this with the ballet slippers, the tennis ball and the jogging shoes, naming each item incorrectly. This will make the children laugh and keep their attention.**

Okay, we have a basketball, ballet slippers, a tennis ball, and jogging shoes. What do these things have in common? *(used in sports)* Are any of these your favorites? *(response)* Which sport do you like the best? *(response)*

Application: I think the toughest of these sports is running. Being a Christian is like being a runner. **Hold up the running shoes.** It requires training and many hours of practice, but we have a lot of people in heaven cheering for us. The Bible calls these people a cloud of witnesses. People like Abraham, Moses, Rahab, David, and lots of others. So always remember that you're not alone when you are running the race of life and trying to do the right things for Jesus. God is with you, and a lot of people are cheering for you!

Let's Pray: Dear Lord, we know that heaven is cheering us on. Give us strength to run the race of life, being faithful to what Jesus wants us to be. Amen.

✝

Proper 16
Luke 13:10-17

Sometimes You Gotta Bend The Rules!

Exegetical Aim: Rules and laws are good. They tell us how we should live our lives, but sometimes there is a greater good to be served by breaking the rules.

Props: Some signs with rules on them. Get some commercially-made signs or just draw them yourself. The contents of the signs are explained below.

Lesson: Good morning! *(response)* I have some signs with me this morning and I want you to read them and tell me who might put up each sign. **Hold up the first sign: No Dogs or Pets Allowed.** What does this sign say? *(response)* Who would put up a sign like this? *(stores)* **Second Sign: STOP.** What does this sign say? *(response)* Who puts up this sign? *(people who make the roads)* **Third sign: No Shirt No Shoes No Service.** What does this sign say? *(response)* Who puts up this sign? *(restaurant)* **Fourth sign: Quiet Please.** What does this sign say? *(response)* Who puts up this sign? *(Librarian)* **Fifth sign: Remember Sunday is holy and you should rest (An adaptation of the Fourth Commandment: Remember the Sabbath and keep it holy).** What does this sign say? *(response)* Who puts up this sign? *(God)*

Signs and rules are very important. They help us know what to do, and some of them even help us know how best to live our lives. But sometimes rules can get in the way of doing something good. Who knows what an ambulance is for? *(response)* And when an ambulance is carrying a sick person to the hospital and they come upon a stop sign **hold up the STOP sign** the ambulance does what? *(response)* That's right. The ambulance goes right through the stop sign. Why does it run right through the stop sign? *(they are in a hurry to get to the hospital, someone's sick)* The stop sign is very important and helps protect us, but sometimes it gets in the way of helping people.

170

Application: Jesus had this very same problem. There was a lady who was crippled. Who knows what "crippled" means? *(response)* That's right. She couldn't walk straight, she was bent over, and she had been this way for eighteen years. The crippled lady came into the church [synagogue] where Jesus was teaching. When Jesus saw the woman, he did something for her. He healed her. Her back straightened and she stood right up! But there were some people there at church who got mad, and they reminded Jesus **hold up the Sabbath sign** that this was Sunday and you're not supposed to do any kind of work on Sunday, including healing. You're supposed to rest. Jesus reminded them that sometimes you've got to work on Sunday. You bend the rules a little because there is a greater good that can be accomplished — like healing someone.

Let's Pray: Father, we know that rules are important, but help us to put people first and not the rules. Amen.

Proper 16
Hebrews 12:18-29

God's Unshakable Kingdom

Exegetical Aim: God's kingdom cannot be shaken.

Props: A baby rattle, a can or plastic jar of un-popped popcorn, and a bottle of water. Bring them out in a box that can be shaken.

Lesson: Today we are going to talk about shaking things. And to help me, I have brought a box that I'm going to shake. **Shake the box.** Can you tell what's inside? *(response)* **Take the rattle out of the box.** Look at this. This is pretty neat. What is it? *(response)* Yes, it's a rattle. This can be shaken, can't it? *(response)* How come I can shake it? *(response)* Is it a very big object? *(response)* **Help them arrive at the answer: "It is small."** Oh, I see. I can shake it because it is small. Even a baby could shake this. **Shake the box again:** Well, what else do you think is in the box? **Repeat the questions with the popcorn and the bottled water. With each item have them arrive at the same conclusion: These things can be shaken due to their size.**

Now I want all of you to stand up and shake something. Come with me. **If it is feasible, lead them over to the wall of the church. If not, then have them hold onto something that is structurally firm and part of the church.** Now I want you all to put your hands on the wall, and on the count of three, we are going to shake the church building. Are you ready? One, two, three! Come on and shake it! **Look around.** Look! What happened? *(nothing, it's not shaking)* Let's try one more time. *(they try to shake the church again)* What's the matter? Can't the church be shaken? *(response)* Why not? *(because it's too big)*

Application: That reminds me. The Bible tells us that God's kingdom, the church, is so big that it cannot be shaken. A little jar of popcorn can be shaken, but not the church. God's kingdom is so big, and powerful nothing can move it. And because it is so big, we

172

do not need to be afraid of anything. We can live just like God wants us to because we trust in something that will not and cannot be shaken. The church will always be here for us, because God will always be here for us.

Let's Pray: Dear God, thank you for giving us a kingdom that is so big that it can't be shaken. Now we know we can live like you want us to live, and you will always be there for us. In Jesus' name, we pray. Amen.

Proper 17
Luke 14:1, 7-14

Kingdom Order

Exegetical Aim: To teach that in God's Kingdom victory does not fall on the strongest and fastest, but on the humble.

Props: First, second, and third place ribbons or trophies. Draw some ribbons if you have nothing commercial.

Lesson: Good morning, children. I have a question for you. Who among you is the fastest? *(response)* And why are you the fastest? *(response)* Who among you is the strongest? *(response)* Why do you think you're the strongest? *(response)* Who among you is the tallest? *(response)* This morning I want to place you in order. We are going to start with the tallest and go down to the littlest. I want you to line up shoulder to shoulder all the way across the altar. **Have them face the congregation and stand shoulder to shoulder making a descending line from tallest to shortest.**

When they are lined up go to the short end and speak to the little ones. Now, who do you think is the tallest child here this morning? *(response)* You think he is? Why? *(response)* Okay, then he probably deserves the first place ribbon. Place the ribbon on the tallest child. **Address the younger ones again:** Now, who do you think is the fastest? *(response)* He's the fastest? Why? *(response)* He probably is the fastest, so we will give him the second place ribbon. **The biggest child should not get all three ribbons. The idea is to give the ribbons to the three tallest children. Address all the children:** I have one ribbon left. Next to these two, who do think is the strongest? *(response)* Why? *(response)* **This ribbon may have to go to number four depending on the make up of the children, but try to get it to number three.**

Application: This is usually what happens: You have a race and the tallest and strongest child always wins. But Jesus told a story that might surprise you. There was a party and whole lot of people showed up for the party. Everybody there was trying to be number one or number two or number three. **As you speak the following words, take the ribbons one by one and place them on the three smallest children. Leave time to walk each ribbon down to the small children. Don't do them all at one time. The symbolism needs to be given time to work.** But Jesus said to them, when you get invited to a party don't try to be number one. Try to be number 13! Try to be the last or least of all the people. Because ... guess what? If you try to get the first place ribbon, it will be taken from you and given to another. And if you try to get the second place ribbon, it will taken from you and given to another, and your third place ribbon will be taken from you and given to another.

What do you think Jesus was trying to tell us? *(response)* It doesn't matter whether we are big or small, whether we are fast or slow, or whether we are strong or weak. What matters is if we care for one another. All of us can help the child who sits by himself at lunch. We can be a friend to the child who gets picked on. All of us can be winners and loved by God if we will take care of those who are in need. Don't always hang out with your friends. Go hang out with someone who needs you as a friend. **Go back to the short end of the line and lay your hands on them — address your comments to the older and bigger.** So remember the little ones. The ones who are not quite as strong as you are. They need to be cared for. **Address all the children:** And God reminds us all to take care of those who don't have any shoes to wear or warm clothes to wear. If you will do this, you will be a winner in God's eyes.

Let's Pray: Lord, help us to be humble and help one another. We don't always have to be number one to be happy. Amen.

Proper 17
Hebrews 13:1-8, 15-16

Bound For Glory

Exegetical Aim: We are bound together by our faith.

Props: A ball of yarn, and a couple of adult or youth helpers.

Lesson: Stand the children in a tight circle. Today we are going to play a little game, but you have to play it quickly, and you have to do just as I say. **Give the ball of yarn to one of the children.** I want you to hold on to the end of the yarn and throw the ball to someone across from you. Now, you hold on to the yarn and pass it to someone else. **Then that person will hold on to the yarn and pass it to someone else. This will continue until you have a web formed in between the children. The adult helpers should help keep the yarn going.** Now what do we have? *(response)* Everyone is connected together.

Watch this ... **Pick someone.** I want you to sit down while the others remain standing. **Have the child sit down.** What happened to the web? *(response)* It went down, didn't it? *(response)* And when it went down, you felt it pull a little, didn't you? *(response)* Can we do anything to help lift him back up? *(response)* That's right. We can lift the web. **Have the child stand up when the web is lifted.**

Application: The Bible tells us that as Christians we are all tied together just like this web. When something happens to one, it affects us, too. There is a scripture in the book of Hebrews that says that we should always be kind to those who are sick or in trouble, because we are all part of the same body. That means that when their web goes down, ours goes down, too. That's when we need to lift their web up, right? *(response)* What are some ways that you can lift someone's web if they are feeling sad? *(response)* What if they are sick, what can we do? *(response)* Let's keep in mind this week that we can lift the web and help someone up who is down or sick.

176

Let's Pray: Gracious God, thank you for putting us all together as Christians, and giving us people to care about. Help us this week to bring cheer to someone who is sad or to help someone who is sick. In Jesus' name. Amen.

Proper 18
Luke 14:25-33

How Much Does It Cost?

Exegetical Aim: Understanding the cost of something before the commitment is made. Key verse: 28.

Props: A toy in its original box, if possible, with a ten-dollar price tag and nine one-dollar bills. Obviously, you can change the original price tag with a sticker to suit this Children's Sermon. The toy could be a football or a Barbie. It does not matter. The prop could also be a candy bar for ten cents and nine pennies. The more desirable the item, the more effective the illustration.

Lesson: With the toy hidden: Good morning! *(response)* We're going to go to the toy store **(or candy store depending on your prop)** this morning and buy a toy. I know exactly what I want; I want this! **Pull out the football.** What is this? *(response)* Yeah, a football. Won't it be great! We can buy this and then take it home and get in the front yard and play football. How many of you have played football? *(response)* Will you play with me if I buy it? *(response)* Good. I wonder how much it costs? *(response)* The price tag has to be around here somewhere? Does anyone see the price tag? *(response)* Oh, it's right here. How much does it cost? *(response)* Ten dollars!? That's a lot of money. I'll have to see how much I have.

    Pull out your wallet or pocketbook and take out the nine one dollar bills. Will you help me count? *(response)* You count them. **Have a child hold out her hand for you to lay the dollar bills into one at a time.** *(One, two, three, four, five, six, seven, eight, nine)* Nine? **In desperation look back in your wallet.** We need ten dollars not nine. Are you sure you counted right? *(response)* We'll count them again. **Take the bills and have them slowly count again.** Only nine dollars! Do you know what that means? *(response)* That's right. I don't have enough money to buy the football and that means we can't play football together. I'm sorry; I thought I had enough money.

Put your dollars back in your wallet and hold it up before them: Next time, before I go to the toy store to buy a toy, what should I do? *(count how much money you have)* **If they say you should ask your parents, respond:** I'm going to buy this toy with my own money. So what do I need to do before I buy the toy? *(response)* I need to count my money, and if I have nine dollars, I can't buy a ten-dollar toy. I need to know how much it costs and how much I have.

Application: The toy store will expect me to have ten dollars if I am going to buy a ten-dollar toy. Jesus said something like that. He said, before we follow God, we need to sit down and think about what that means and how much it's going to "cost us" to follow him. What do you think it costs to follow God? *(response)* **Give the children time to answer. If they answer with a monetary figure:** It will cost more than our money to follow God. What do you think it costs to follow God? *(response)* **Guide them toward appropriate answers.** It will actually cost us our lives! Everything we have and everything we own — even everything we are and want to do. Can you believe that? We have to give everything to God: our money, our family, our talents, our toys, our friends, and our love. That's what it costs to follow God. Jesus told us to make sure we are ready to pay that price before we come to God, because God expects nothing less.

Let's Pray: Lord, whatever it costs, we are ready to pay the price to follow you. Amen.

Proper 18
Philemon 1-21

Ask Nicely

Exegetical Aim: Our requests of others should be polite. We should use kindness whenever possible.

Props: A bottle of vinegar, an onion, a jar of jelly, and a packet of Kool-Aid.

Lesson: Today I want to take a survey to see what kind of things you like, okay? **Hold up the jar of vinegar.** How many know what this is? *(response)* Now, how many people like to have a big, cold glass of vinegar on a warm summer's day? *(response)* No? **Hold up the Kool-Aid pouch.** Well, who would rather have a drink made from this? *(response)* So you would rather have the Kool-Aid than the vinegar? *(response)* Okay.

Next, how many of you would like just to open up your mouth and bite into this? **Hold up the onion.** *(response)* No? Well, what about this? **Hold up the jar of jelly.** You would rather have the jelly. Hmmm. Why would you rather have the jelly and the Kool-Aid than the onion and the vinegar? *(response)* Oh, I see. Because they are sweeter.

Now set the jelly down a few feet away. I would like for one of you to get up and get that jelly for me, but before you do, I need to ask you something. Would you rather I use a deep voice **lower your voice,** and a mean face **make a mean face,** and point at you **point,** and order you to get the jelly? Or would you rather I speak kindly and ask you to please get me the jelly? Which would you rather I do? *(ask nicely)* Why? *(response)* Oh, I see. It is a nicer and sweeter way to ask that way. Let's try it. **Turn to one of the children.** Would you please get the jelly for me? **When the child returns with the jelly, say, "Thank you."** I'd much rather have jelly people around me than vinegary people.

Application: In the Bible a man named Paul asked his friend Philemon to do something for him. He said, "Philemon, I could order you to do this, but I am going to ask nicely." Why do you think he did that? *(response)* Yes, Paul knew that Philemon would likely respond to niceness than to an order. In the same way, we must be nice to our friends and classmates in school. When we need something we have to be polite out of love for that person, and never demanding or ordering. It's much sweeter, right? *(response)*

Let's Pray: Gracious God, help us to be nice this week and ask please. In Jesus' name. Amen.

Proper 19
Luke 15:1-10

The Lost Sheep

Exegetical Aim: God's love and concern for one lost child.

Props: A child who is able to play along with hiding until she is found. It should be a child who is known by most of the other children. Just before the children's sermon the child hiding should take her place. You want the children to create as much commotion in the sanctuary as possible, so arrange for her to find a good hiding place. Gather the children as usual.

Lesson: Good morning! *(response)* It's good to have everybody here this morning ... Wait a minute ... Is everybody here? *(response)* Somebody is missing. *(response)* Who is missing? *(response)* **If they don't know, describe the child.** You know what we have to do when someone is lost? *(response)* That's right. We need to find [child's name] and bring her back. **Get up and motion for the children to get up as you say:** Let's go find [Child's name].

Good job! You found her. Boy, [Child's name]! We thought we would never find you. Have any of you ever been lost? *(response)* What happened? *(response)* Who found you? *(response)* It's scary when you get lost, isn't it? *(response)*

Application: This reminds me of a story Jesus told. He said there was this shepherd who had a hundred sheep and he lost one of them. Do you know what the shepherd did? *(response)* That's right. He left all his sheep and went after the lost one, and he didn't stop until he had found that lost sheep. Jesus was talking about you and me. Whenever we are lost, God will come after us and he will keep searching until he finds us.

Let's Pray: Lord, you are our shepherd, and you come looking for us when we are lost. Amen.

✝

Proper 19
1 Timothy 1:12-17

Saving Grace

Exegetical Aim: To show that Christ is our salvation.

Props: A life-preserver (vest), arm floats for a child, an inflatable ring, sunglasses, etc.

Lesson: Hey, kids, it's not going to be warm much longer, so I'm going to go swimming. I just thought I would bring some of my things to show you. Do you think these things will help me swim? **Put on the gear and put the arm floats on for a laugh. Put on the sunglasses as a finishing touch.**

For what do we use these things? *(response)* One of these things can even save our lives. Which one of these is the most important? *(they point to the life preserver)* What do you call this? *(response)* It is called a life preserver. Whenever we are in a boat or canoe, we should always wear one of these. If my boat turned over and I fell in the water, what would happen to me? *(response)*

Application: You know, that reminds me of a scripture in the Bible. It says that Jesus Christ came into the world to save us, to be a life preserver. A life preserver like the one I'm wearing has been specially made to help me stay above the water, but Jesus is a different kind of life saver. How does Jesus save us? *(response)* Jesus died on a cross to save us from sin and death. You see, we are all sinners (that means we all do bad things), and Jesus saves us from those bad things — he forgives us. Whenever you think you're getting into trouble, you can pray and trust that Jesus will be there with you to save you. He will do that because he really cares for you. Here is the verse from the Bible, and I want you to say it with me: Christ *(Christ)* came into the world *(came into the world)* to save sinners *(to save sinners)*.

Let's Pray: Dear God, thank you for sending Jesus Christ to save us and to care for us. For we pray in his name. Amen.

Proper 20
Luke 16:1-13

Take Care Of Your Wagon

Exegetical Aim: If you take care of your toys today you will be entrusted with greater things tomorrow. Stewardship is a sign of character. Key verses: 10-11.

Props: A child's red wagon or a tricycle or a small bike.

Lesson: The children should gather around the wagon. Good morning! *(response)* How many of you would like to drive your mom's or dad's car? *(response)* Where would you go if you could drive the car? *(response)* When you get a little older, you might be able to do that, but first you have do something for me. **Lay your hands on the wagon:** If you take care of this wagon — I mean really take good care of it — then you can drive the car. **Pause.** Do you know why I am saying that? *(response)*

I am saying that because what you do now is an indication of the kind of person you will be when you grow up. If you tear up your wagon and your tricycle and your bicycle, it means you will probably tear up the family car. Your mom and dad need to know they can trust you. They need to know that you will take care of things they give you today before they will allow you to drive something as important as the family car.

Application: Jesus said something just like this. He said, "Whoever can be trusted with little things **indicate the wagon by taking hold of it** can be trusted with ..." What? *(big things)* That's right. That's exactly what Jesus said: "Whoever can be trusted with little things can be trusted with big things." It's not only true with our wagons and cars; it's true of life as well. If you share your toys now, then you will probably be a generous and giving person when you grow up. If you love your brother and your sister and your friends, then you will probably be a good husband or wife when you grow up. The way we behave now is a strong indication of who we will be when get older. Take care of your toys **hold the wagon again** and one day you'll drive the family car!

Let's Pray: Lord, help us. We know that we need to take care of the little things, before you will trust us with big things. Amen.

Proper 20
1 Timothy 2:1-7

Mediating The Lesson

Exegetical Aim: To show that there is one God, and one mediator between God and man.

Props: One child with whom you have discussed beforehand that he/she is to be a mediator.

Lesson: Place all of the children together, except for the one child. The one child needs to sit by you. Don't say anything at all to the other children. You will whisper instructions to the mediator who will then relay them to the children.

1. Whisper: Please sit quietly.

2. Whisper: Would you like to play a game? *(response)*

3. Whisper: We are playing a game called Mediation.

4. Whisper: Guess what "mediation" means? *(response)* **As the children guess, only whisper a yes or no to the child. He/she in turn will give your answer to the children. Give them some time to define the term. If they need help, whisper to the mediator:** We are playing the game right now.

Application: Now I will talk for a while. How do you like the game? *(response)* I didn't say a word to you directly, but you still knew exactly what I said because [child's name] was very good at telling you what I said. That's what a mediator is. Someone who works between us.

Did you know that Jesus was a mediator? He was a mediator between God and ... who? *(us)* Jesus spoke to us about who God is. Although we can't see God, we know what he wants because Jesus tells us. **For the older children you might add:** Let me ask you a question. What was the only way for you to know what I was saying? *(through [Child's name])* Now, what's the only way to know what God is saying to us? *(through Jesus)* So always look to Jesus to know God's will. We can never go wrong if we do what Jesus, our mediator to God, tells us.

Let's Pray: Dear God, thank you for Jesus who is our mediator, and who shows us the way to you. In his name we pray. Amen.

Proper 21
Luke 16:19-31

Richie Rich

Exegetical Aim: We must show concern and care for others.

Props: Photographs of children who are shoeless, shirtless, and hungry.

Lesson: Good morning! *(response)* How many of you have shoes on this morning? *(response)* How many of you have dirty socks on? *(response)* Just checking. I wonder how many shoes we have here. Let's count them. Everyone stick out your shoes. Count with me. **Count the shoes.** There are 26 shoes here this morning. I have a photograph here of some children in Latin America. How many shoes do you see in this picture. Look closely and count them. *(none — they don't have any shoes)* Why don't they have any? *(because they are poor)*

How many shirts do we have here this morning? Let's count them. Count with me. **Count the shirts.** We have twelve shirts. I have another picture of some children in Africa. How many shirts do you see in this picture? *(in your photo there may be two of six that have a shirt)* Why are these children without shirts? *(they're poor)*

What did you have for breakfast? *(response)* What did you have to drink? *(response)* **As another counting exercise, count the number of eggs, pancakes, and orange juices the children consumed.** I have one more picture to show you. Look at these boys and girls. **This should be a photo of children suffering malnutrition.** What do you see? *(response)* How many eggs do you think these children had this morning? *(response)* How many pancakes? *(response)* Do you think they had any orange juice? *(response)* That's sad, isn't it? *(response)*

Additional prop: For churches too limited in resources to accomplish this additional prop, please skip this paragraph. Have

189

a child enter the sanctuary in a battery-powered car and stop before the children. The child should be well dressed and wearing sunglasses and jewelry. Getting out of the car, the child will say, "Hello, everyone! Sorry I am late for church, but I was waiting for my cell phone to charge. **Pause.** What are you doing? *(response)* Hey! Look at those photographs of those kids. They really need to put some clothes on. **At this time the cell phone is rung by a person in the vestibule. If a phone line is not available, use another cell phone to place the call. Answering the phone, the child says,** "What? Your kidding? Okay. All right. Sorry, I've got to go. See ya 'round." **Getting back in the car, the child drives out of the sanctuary. Watch in silence as the car exits. Speak to the children about what just happened.** What was that? *(response)* What did he say about these people in the picture? *(response)* Do you think he noticed that they were poor? *(response)* Why didn't he notice? *(response)*

Application: Jesus told a story about a man who was very rich who lived in luxury every day, and outside the man's house at the gate was a man who was very poor and starved every day for something to eat. Even the dogs would come up and lick the sores on this poor man's body. Jesus said the rich man never helped the poor man. **[This can be inferred from the passage. Jesus did not explicitly say this.]** What do you think happened to them when they died? *(response)* The rich man was punished and the poor man was comforted. It is very important to love and care for people, especially those who are hungry and sick. That's the kind of people that God wants us to be.

Let's Pray: Father, we don't want to ignore people who are sick and hungry. Teach us to be tenderhearted and to reach out to those who need shoes, clothes, and food. Amen.

Proper 21
1 Timothy 6:6-19

Storing Up The Good

Exegetical Aim: To demonstrate "storing up for themselves the treasure of a good foundation." (v. 19)

Props: A cup of water, a cup of coffee with some grounds, two coffee filters, and a pitcher.

Lesson: Today we are going to do an experiment. **Hold up the cup of water.** What do I have here? *(response)* Yes, it is water. I'm going to pour this water through this filter and into the pitcher. After I am done, I want you to tell me if there is anything remaining on the filter. **Pour the water through the filter and into the pitcher.** Do you think the water left anything on the filter? *(response)* Look at it. What do you see? Do you see anything other than a little wetness on the filter? *(response)* No? Hmmm, what do you know? **Do the exact same thing with the cup of coffee. After questioning the children, pour the coffee and grounds into the pitcher through the filter.** Before I show you the filter, what do you think is on it? Will I find water? *(response)* No? I won't find water? Let's look at the filter and see what is left. Ooh, look at the leftover coffee. There's some of the grounds. Does that look good? *(response)*

Application: Which of the liquids left the cleanest filter? *(response)* The water, right? Why? *(response)* Yes, because whatever goes into the filter leaves a trace of itself. If you pour something clean through the filter, the filter will remain clean. If you pour coffee that is dark and has grounds, it will leave the filter dark and with grounds. The same thing is true in your life. If a person has badness inside of him, what will come out of that person? *(response)* You are correct; badness will come out of that person, just like the grounds inside of that coffee are left behind in the filter. But if a person is good and puts good things inside of oneself, like prayer, and good

191

manners, and love, and respect, then what will come out of that person? *(response)* Goodness will come out, just as the water that was clean and didn't leave any other particles in the filter. The Apostle Paul told us to store up good things in our lives, so that we might enjoy eternal life. Let's only put good things in our lives, so that only good things will come out.

Let's Pray: Dear God, thank you for giving us so many good things in life. Help us to act good, to love Jesus, and to pray so that we can store up goodness inside. That way, we may enjoy eternal life and let only good things come out of our lives. In Jesus' name, we pray. Amen.

Proper 22
Luke 17:3-10

A Little Forgiveness Goes A Long Way

Exegetical Aim: We do not need a lot of faith to exercise forgiveness. My understanding of this passage comes from combining the meaning of verses 4-6 and 10. Basically, it is our duty as disciples to forgive — and this I think is Jesus' understanding of faith. The disciples understand this and respond in verse 5 with a request to help them have enough faith to forgive so generously.

Props: Acorns or seeds from a traditionally large tree and a bowl that can be covered. Enough seeds for each child.

Lesson: Good morning! *(response)* I have something in this bowl and it's really, really big. Does any one know what it is? *(response)* No, that's not it. I'll give you another hint. It's bigger than a car. *(response)* No, you still haven't guessed what's in the bowl. I'll give you one more hint. It's bigger than a house. *(response: it can't be bigger than a house)* I promise. I'm not lying to you. It really is bigger than a house. Do you know what it is? *(response)*

   Uncover the bowl and hold it just above eye level. All of you reach in and take one. What is it? *(response)* Is it bigger than a house? *(response)* Well, not right now, but one day it will be. Do you know what kind of seed that is? *(response)* It is an oak tree seed. One day that little seed you are holding in your hand will be bigger than a car; it will be bigger than a house; it fact, it will be big enough to build a tree house in it. So now do you believe me? *(response)* It is bigger than a house, isn't it? *(response)*

Application: This seed reminds me of something Jesus said. He said, "If your brother or your sister hurts you, forgive him every time, even if he hurts you seven times!" He said, "Forgiveness is like a small seed. When it is planted, it can grow to an enormous size." Just a little forgiveness given to your brother, or given to your sister, or given to your friend can grow to be bigger than a car

193

and bigger than a house. Do you know what actually grows when you plant forgiveness? *(response)* Love and compassion. So, let's ask Jesus to give us just a little bit of faith to forgive one another, and then we'll watch how love grows! Maybe it will get so big we can build a home in it.

Let's Pray: Father, we forgive one another. Teach us to let go of bitterness and anger so that your love can grow. Amen.

Proper 22
2 Timothy 1:1-14

Calling All Persons

Exegetical Aim: God's call is not dependent on what we do or who we are, but upon God's love and purposes.

Props: None.

Lesson: When the children arrive down front, ask them to go back toward their seats until they hear your instructions. When about half of them have arrived at their seats, say, Come back, come back, hurry! Now you can sit down. **Ask one of the children,** Where were you standing when I called you? *(response)* **Now ask another,** Where were you when you heard the call? *(response)* **Ask a couple of other children the same two questions.**

Application: All of you were in different places, walking in different directions. Why were you in different places? *(response)* Oh, because you don't sit in the same place. Who heard me call? *(response)* All of you heard me call? *(response)*

I want you to know something. For the rest of your life it will not matter where you are if God calls you. Whether you are at home or at school, whether you are seven years old or seventy years old, God will be calling you because he loves you and has a purpose for your lives. His purpose is for all of us to know Jesus.

So always remember that no matter where you are, or who you are, or how big you are, or how small you are, or if you like sports, or if you like books, or if you are red, yellow, black, or white, God calls us all to come to him and to know his Son Jesus Christ. And we must be willing to come to him when he calls.

Let's Pray: Dear God, thank you for calling us all to know Jesus Christ as our Savior, no matter who we are or what we do. Amen.

✝

Proper 23
Luke 17:11-19

Thankful For The Little Things

Exegetical Aim: Appreciation for the little things.

Props: A medium to oversized box, a tooth brush, a pair of tennis shoes, a book, and a regular kitchen plate. If these items can be placed in the box and gift wrapped, it will create greater anticipation, but it is not necessary.

Lesson: Good morning! *(response)* I have some gifts for you this morning and I am so excited about giving them to you. You don't have any of these and you're going to like them. Can you help me open the present? **If you have wrapped the box, allow the children to assist, but don't let them see the contents. Opening the box and looking inside:** Okay, I bet you don't have any of these neat presents and you're going to be so surprised. Let's see what we have in here. Here it is! **Pull out the tooth brush:** A toothbrush, isn't that great? You know what you do with this? **Act like you are brushing your teeth.** You clean your teeth like this. I bet none of you have a tooth brush. *(response)* What? *(response)* You all have tooth brushes? *(response)* Well, how did you all get tooth brushes? *(at the store)* Who bought them for you? *(mom, parents)* You have very special parents. You know what I think you should do? You should say, "Thank you," to your mom and dad for the toothbrush.

   Looking back in the box: Okay, let's see what else we have. I know. You don't have a pair of **pull out the tennis shoes** these! These are great. You put them on your feet and you can run really fast. *(response)* What? *(response)* You all have tennis shoes? *(response)* Well, how did you all get tennis shoes? *(got them at the store)* Who bought them for you? *(mom)* You have very special parents. You know what I think you should do? You should say, "Thank you," to your mom and dad for your tennis shoes.

196

All right. I bet you don't have one of **pull out the book** these. Now this is something here; you can read a story about other people and what they did. *(response)* Oh, no. You have one of these too? All right then, I've got this one last present. **Pull out the plate.** This is neat. You can put your food on it and you don't have to eat off the ground. *(response)* You have one of these too? *(response)*

Application: With the objects out before the children: Do you know that there are children all over the world who do not have a toothbrush, or a book to read, or a plate to eat on? They don't even have tennis shoes. You should be very grateful and tell your parents, "Thank you." They've given you so much. There's a story in the Bible where Jesus healed ten men who were really sick and only one of them said, "Thank you," to Jesus. The other nine just walked away. I want you to be thankful children. The next time something is done for you or bought for you, even if it's a toothbrush, what are you going to say? *(Thank you!)* Good!

Let's Pray: Oh, God, make us grateful. We thank you not only for the big things but for the toothbrushes, dinner plates, and daily bread. Amen.

Proper 23
2 Timothy 2:8-15

Lifting Hands

Exegetical Aim: The need for prayer.

Props: None needed.

Lesson: How many hands do we have here today? Raise your hands and let me count them. **Count the hands.** Twenty-four hands. Wow, that's a lot of hands! What are some reasons people raise their hands? *(to ask a question)* Can you name any other reasons? *(response)* Did you know that people can even raise their hands in anger? *(response)* Can you tell me how people raise their hands in anger? What do they do with their hands? *(make a fist)* **Put your hands in a boxing position and gently jab at the air a couple of times.** Sometimes we raise our hands because we are yelling. **Wave your hands slightly above your head and let out a quiet scream to create a bit of levity.** But there is one other reason why people raise their hands. **Put your hands in a prayer position. The children will most likely say, "To pray."** That's right. We also can lift our hands in prayer.

Application: A long time ago the Apostle Paul told the church to lift up hands in prayer and not in anger. What do you think he meant by that? Which is better, praying or fighting? *(response)* Yes, that is right. It is better to pray than to fight. The Apostle Paul knew that if our hands were busy praying, then we couldn't use them to fight. So the next time you are angry and you feel like **make a fist** hitting somebody, remember instead to do what with your hands? **Move your hands into the position of prayer.** *(response)* That is correct. Lift them in prayer.

Let's Pray: Thank you, Father, for giving us our hands for many good things. Help us to remember never to lift them in anger, and instead to lift them in prayer to you. In Jesus' name. Amen.

Proper 24
Luke 18:1-8

Stick-to-it-tiveness

Exegetical Aim: Practice won't make you perfect, but persistence will surely get you closer to your goal.

Props: A musical instrument you do not know how to play. A guitar is used here.

Lesson: Good morning! *(response)* What is this I have in my hand? *(a guitar)* That's right. Does anyone know how to play the guitar? *(response)* **Point to one of the strings:** Do you know what string this is? *(response)* **Pluck the string so that it sounds out.** Do you want to know what string this is? *(yes)* Well, you will have to ask someone else because I have no idea. I wish I knew a little bit more about the guitar. **Pause and look at the instrument.** It's a beautiful thing, isn't it? How can I learn to play the guitar? *(lessons)* After I take lessons, then what will I have to do? *(practice)* Let me try and make a chord. **Make a chord and strum it. The idea here is to produce a horrible sound.** How many times do you think I would have to practice? *(a lot)* What if I practiced one time? Would that be enough? *(no)* **Try to play the chord once more.** I think you're right. It's going to take more than just one practice session.

Application: You know, if you want to accomplish anything you have to stick to it. I call it Stick-to-it-tiveness. This guitar is a lot like school. If you want to make good grades, what do you need to do? *(study)* How many times do you need to study? *(bunch)* This guitar is also a lot like baseball. If you want to be a good batter, what do you need to do? *(practice)* How many balls do you need to hit? *(response)* This guitar is even a lot like our relationship with God. Can anyone tell me how this guitar is a lot like our relationship with God? *(who knows what the response will be to this)* Jesus taught us that we should always pray and not give up. It's very important that we pray, but it is also very important that we never give up in our prayers. We need to have Stick-to-it-tiveness!

Let's Pray: Lord, I pray for these children that you will help them practice their math and their reading, and help me with **play the chord once more** the guitar. But most of all, help us always to pray and never give up. Amen.

Optional: If you know how to play an instrument, fake your lack of skills and after the prayer start playing the instrument.

Proper 24
2 Timothy 3:14—4:5

Building Blocks

Exegetical Aim: To demonstrate the Bible's gift of instruction.

Props: 1) Children's building toys (Lego's, Tinkertoys) and the instruction booklet that shows different building designs. 2) Pre-make one of the simple designs (ship, car, etc.) except for one last crucial and obvious part. You will "need" the instructions for this part.

Lesson: Who likes to play with building blocks? *(response)* So do I, and I was up in my office all week long building things. One thing I really like to build is cars. I have always been fascinated by cars. Would you like to see a car I've almost finished? **Bring out the almost finished car.** What do you think about it? *(response)* It needs something else but I can't figure out what it is. How can I find out what it needs? Is there something I can look at to tell me what is missing? *(response)* Is there some kind of book that will help me? *(instructions, directions)* Oh, an instruction booklet. Well, I have one right here. And here's what I'm building. **Show the picture to the children.** According to the design, I just need to add one more thing. Can you help me find it? *(children should help you search in the box for the missing piece)* **Now add the missing part.** Hey! That's it! Now it's finished because I used the instructions.

Application: Hold up the Bible. I have another kind of instruction book. What do we build from this instruction book? *(response)* That's right, the Bible is our instruction book for living. In fact, Saint Paul once said that scripture is inspired by God and useful for instruction in life. Wow! That means that God has given us the Bible as a book by which to live! So, if we want to know how to build a car out of blocks we look at the...? *(response)*

202

Right, the instructions. And if we have a question about how to build our lives, we read the ...? *(response)* Yes, the Bible.

Let's Pray: Dear God, thank you for giving us the Bible to instruct us how to live good lives. In the name of Jesus Christ, we pray. Amen.

Proper 25
Luke 18:9-14

Oh, Lord, It's Hard To Be Humble

Exegetical Aim: To teach humility before God in prayer.

Props: None.

Lesson: Usually when we gather up here, we talk to one another about different things, but this morning I'd really like to pray, but I need you to help me. Would you help me pray? *(response)* Good, let's pray: **As you pray fold your hands, look up to heaven, and pray in a prideful manner.** "God, I thank you that I'm not like other boys and girls. They're all a bunch of brats, they are mean and nasty, and they lie all the time. God, I thank you I'm better than those other boys and girls; I am so good because I give my money to the church. Amen." Well? **Pause and look around at the children, expressing a desire for a response about how you did in your prayer. If no response is given, ask them for one:** How did I do? *(response)* What was wrong with that? *(no)* Why? *(response)* You mean I shouldn't say that other boys and girls are mean and nasty and call them a bunch of brats? *(no)* Can you tell me how I should pray? *(response)* What else can I say? *(response)*

Okay, let me try it again. Would you help me pray again? *(response)* Oh, thanks, you've been so much help! Let's pray again: **Bow your head and humbly pray** "God, please forgive me, I am a sinner. I am not always nice to people and sometimes I'm mean to my mom and my dad and my brothers and sisters and friends, and I say things I shouldn't say. Please forgive me." Well? *(response)* How did I do this time? *(response)* Why is that way right and the other way wrong? *(response)*

Application: Does anyone know what being humble means? *(response)* It means not looking down on other people. We are not supposed to think that we are better than everyone else. Being humble means putting ourselves last and putting others first and asking God for forgiveness. It's very important to be humble because Jesus said, "He who looks down on people will be brought down himself, and he who humbles himself will be lifted up." What do you think Jesus meant by that? *(response)* That's right. God will forgive those who are humble, but he will not forgive those who are proud. Thanks for helping me with my prayers. I'll try to be humble so God will forgive me.

Let's Pray: Oh, Lord, it's hard to be humble, but none of us are perfect. Only you are perfect. Teach us to be humble. Amen.

Proper 25
2 Timothy 4:6-8, 16-18

Crown Of Righteousness

Exegetical Aim: To demonstrate that there are rewards for our faithfulness.

Props: A trophy, a medal or certificate of achievement, and construction paper crowns. To make the crowns: Cut V's across the top of the construction paper. Then round the construction paper together and tape it. Make sure you have enough for every child. You should keep the crowns hidden from sight until the end.

Lesson: Have you ever been in a race and received an award for winning? *(response)* How about getting a certificate for being good in a subject at school? *(response)* **Adapt the following as it pertains to you:** Let me show you something that I received. **Show them the trophy.** When I was younger, I was on a basketball team and I got this trophy at the end of the year. And when I was in high school, I did so well in math that I received this medal. But I want to talk to you about people a long time ago. In the ancient world, when people would race each other, the person who won didn't get a trophy or a medal or a certificate. **Pull one of the paper crowns out and put it on your head.** The person who won the race received a special crown. And whenever the winner wore the crown, everyone knew that the person had done a great job.

Application: The Apostle Paul liked to go to these games and he remembered seeing athletes receive crowns for winning the race. He said, "That's the way it's going to be for us when we finally see God. He is going to give us a crown of righteousness." What is a crown of righteousness? *(responses, if any)* It's the prize we are going to receive from God for doing good things and trusting in him. Today I want to give each of you one of these crowns. **Pass out the crowns.** And whenever you wear it, I don't want you to pretend to be a king or a queen. I want you to remember that this crown is to remind you to do what God wants you to do. Take it to your parents, and tell them what kind of crown it is: a crown of righteousness.

Let's Pray: Oh, Father, we thank you that when we see you some-day, you will remember us in a wonderful way. Help us to do all that you want us to do, in the name of Jesus Christ. Amen.

All Saints' Sunday
Luke 6:20-31

The Golden Rule

Exegetical Aim: Treating others the way we want to be treated.

Props: Wear shoes with laces.

Lesson: Start this sermon conveying an agitated state. Okay, I don't want anyone poking me, because I don't like being poked. Okay? *(response)* Good. **Fold your arms and harrumph. Wait a few seconds and reach over and poke one of the older children on the arm. Then fold your arms again. Allow some time for this to sink in. If no one says anything or does anything, reach over and poke another one of the older children and wait again. If someone pokes you, do the next three sentences. If no one pokes you, then skip the next three sentences.** Hey! I told you I don't want anyone poking me. Why did you poke me? *(response)* But I told you not to poke me.

And another thing. I don't want anyone **reach down and hold your shoe laces** untying my shoelaces. Okay? *(response)* That really bothers me when someone unties my shoes. **Wait a moment in the guarded position and then reach over to the nearest shoes and untie them. Repeat with silence and the untying of another pair of shoes. After the second pair, raise up and do a "gotcha" laugh at the person whose shoes you just untied. If someone unties your shoes, do the next three sentences. If no one unties your shoes, then skip the next three sentences.** Hey! I told you not to untie my shoes. Why did you do that? *(response)* But I told you not to untie my shoes. *(response)*

Application: It is hoped by this point the children are arguing against your inconsistencies. Use it as the transition. Oh, I see. I should treat you the same way I want you to treat me. Do you know what that is called? *(response)* That's called the Golden Rule and Jesus is the one who said it. He said, "Do to others as you would have them do to you." Do you know that if we would follow that one little rule, it would change our lives? We would no longer argue. We would no longer poke one another. We would seldom ever fight. And, I think that our shoes **look down at your untied shoes** would stay tied all day long.

Let's Pray: Lord, help us to live by your Golden Rule and to treat others as we would like them to treat us. Amen.

All Saints' Sunday
Ephesians 1:11-23

The Trust Fall

Exegetical Aim: God's promise of salvation and our need to trust in his word. Key verse: 13.

Props: Some small stickers or a hand stamp.

Lesson: When I was younger, I went to camp. One thing that camp did was teach me how to trust. What does trust mean? **Work with the children on this for a moment.** One way that I learned how to trust was by doing something called a "trust fall." We climbed a tree about six feet off the ground. We would stand facing the tree, and then we would fall backward off of the tree, and everyone would catch us. Does that sound scary? *(response)* I know it does. It was scary for me. Well, after we fell backwards and were caught, we would get a stamp on our hands to remind us of what we had just accomplished. Would anyone like to do the trust fall? **Choose a child whom you can easily stop from falling.** Instead of climbing a tree, I just want you to stand and fall backwards. I promise I will not let you fall to the ground. **Coax the child into falling backwards. Catch him/her almost immediately. If you have steps at the altar, have the child stand on one the first steps.**

Application: Now give the child a stamp or a sticker on the hand. This stamp is to remind you how well you did. You trusted me, and because you trusted me, I was able to catch you and not let you fall. **At this point, other children will want to do this. Tell them that after church, you will catch them, too, and give them stickers.** The Bible tells us something like this about God. The Apostle Paul said that "you trusted in God ... and then you were sealed with the Spirit of promise." When we trust God for our salvation, he will never let us down. And then he will give us a seal to remind us that we belong to God. And that seal is the Holy Spirit. And just like the sticker on your hand, the Holy Spirit will remind us that we can trust God. So remember always to trust God for your salvation, and remember that salvation comes through Jesus Christ. When you believe in Jesus Christ, God will seal you with his Spirit. **Motion with your hand as if you were putting a sticker on your heart.**

Let's Pray: Almighty God, thank you for saving us through Jesus Christ, and thank you for giving your Holy Spirit to help us remember to trust in you. Amen.

Proper 26
Luke 19:1-10

Little Big Man

Exegetical Aim: How to be big in God's eyes.

Props: Measuring tape.

Lesson: Good morning! *(response)* I have a question for you this morning. How many of you are short? *(response)* Why do you feel short? *(response)* I wonder who is the shortest. **Hold out the tape measure.** What is this? *(tape measure)* Let's find out who is the shortest. Everybody stand up. **Here are two ways to proceed: 1. Measure each child, leaving the shortest for last. 2. If you have too many children to measure individually, then measure five feet from the ground and slowly decrease the height of the tape.** Are any of you this tall? *(response)* How many are this tall? *(response)* And so on. **Have the shortest sit beside you.**

[Name of child] is the shortest. She is two feet eleven inches. Did you know that there is a story in the Bible about a short man who was big in God's eyes. Does anyone know his name? *(Zacchaeus)* That's right. His name was Zacchaeus, and one day, as Jesus entered the city of Jericho, there was a crowd of people around Jesus. Zacchaeus, being a short man, couldn't see Jesus. What do you do when you can't see over people? *(response)* He was jumping up and down but he just couldn't see over that crowd. What would you do if you were trying to see Jesus, but you couldn't see him because of a big crowd. *(climb)* Do you know what Zacchaeus did? *(climbed)* That's right. He ran down the street and he climbed up a sycamore fig tree.

Well, when Jesus walked by, he saw old Zacchaeus up in the sycamore fig tree. He said, "Zacchaeus, come down from there right now and take me to your house. I am going to have dinner with you." Do you know what Zacchaeus said to Jesus as they were eating dinner together? *(response)* He said, "Look, Lord! Here and

212

now I give half of everything I own to the poor, and if I have cheated anybody, I will pay them pack four times what I took."

Application: Do you know what Jesus said? *(response)* Well, this impressed Jesus so much, he said, "Today salvation has come to this house. This man is a Son of Abraham." I want you to know something. It doesn't matter if you are short, skinny, or weak. You can be big in God's eyes if you will do as Zacchaeus has done. Help others and be honest.

Let's Pray: God, we know that even little people can do great things. Use these little ones to do your will in this world. Amen.

[Another method of conveying the story without actually measuring is to stand the children together in a crowded fashion and put the smallest in the back so they cannot see. While you sit down and tell the story, try to interact with the small ones. After you have told the Zacchaeus story, allow the small ones to come up front and ask them how they felt. Let them know that small children can be big in God's eyes if they will do as Zacchaeus has done.]

Proper 26
2 Thessalonians 1:1-4 (11-12)

Increasing Love

Exegetical Aim: The need for increasing love in our hearts.

Props: Balloons that have not been inflated and a box large enough to cover inflated balloons.

Lesson: Bring the large box with the deflated balloons with you, acting as if you are being very careful. I want to show you something this morning that I have brought with me. I believe that you will like what I have brought. Do you want to know what it is? *(response)* It's balloons — beautiful, different colored, balloons! Do you want to see them? *(response)* Of course you do! Who wouldn't want to see balloons? I have them here in my box. Are you ready? *(response)* Here goes! **Carefully open the box and act as if the balloons are going to fly out. After opening the box, look inside.** There they are, my beautiful balloons. **Reach inside and pull out one of the deflated balloons.** This is one of my favorite colors for a balloon. Isn't it pretty? *(response)* You don't sound very excited about my balloons. What's the matter? *(response)* Oh, you thought the balloons were going to be blown up. Do you think the balloons will be prettier blown up? *(response)* Let's see if you are right. **Blow up the balloon a small amount.** How's that? Is that good? *(no)* No? Let's try some more. **Now half way.** How about now? *(no)* No? Okay, I'll try one more time. **Completely blow up the balloon and tie it.** I think you are right. The more the air increased inside, the prettier it became.

Application: The Apostle Paul said this about Christians. In the Bible, Paul tells a church that he is thankful that they are increasing in their love for one another. He knew that the more love increases in our hearts, the better off we are. Which is the better balloon? **Hold up the inflated and a deflated balloon.** Is it the one with no air or the one with a lot of air inside of it? *(the one* *blown up)* You are right. The balloon with the air is better. In the same way, the more love we have in our hearts, the better we are at living. Without love in our hearts, we are flat and useless. **Hold up the empty balloon.** But with love ever increasing in our hearts, we can soar to new heights, **gently tap the filled balloon high into the air,** and be what God intended us to be — a useful loving person. So the next time you see a balloon, remember to fill your hearts with love, just as a balloon is filled with air.

Let's Pray: Thank you, dear Father, that you love us, and that you allow love to fill our hearts. In Jesus' name, we pray. Amen.

Proper 27
Luke 20:27-38

Big Changes

Exegetical Aim: As we grow in life and as we grow with God, we will always have to deal with changes. Sometimes it means letting go of the old and accepting the new. Heaven will bring about the biggest of these changes.

Props: A diaper, wipes, a baby bottle (or a jar of baby food and a baby spoon), and a pacifier.

Lesson: I have something this morning I think you need. **Hold up the diaper.** Okay, who needs his diaper changed? *(response)* All right, don't be shy. Who needs his diaper changed? Anyone have wet britches? *(response)* I even brought the wipes. What? *(response)* What do you mean you don't wear diapers? *(response)* **Ignore their statements about being grown-up.** Well, then, here's something you need ... a bottle. Okay, who is hungry? Who needs his bottle? *(response)* What? *(response)* But you use a bottle all the time. *(response)* All right, no bottle. Here's something you can use. *(response)* You mean you don't even use pacifiers anymore? *(response)* Why not ... you used to use them all the time? *(response)* You're grown up? *(response)* How old are you now? *(response)* Tell me what growing up has to do with no longer wearing diapers and no longer eating baby food. How come you no longer need these things? *(response)* **Keep the pacifier in your hands as you speak with the children.**

Application: My, how you've grown! It's sad sometimes to let go of diapers, bottles, and pacifiers, but it means we are doing some new things. Tell me some things you can do now that you are big boys and big girls? *(response)* What else can you do now that you are big? *(response)* Let me ask you a question: Do you miss the diapers? *(response)* Why don't you miss them? *(response)* I understand. **Pause.** Are you sure none of you would like to wear the diaper? *(no!)* **If there is a wise guy who takes you up on it, motion him to come over. He'll back down.**

Jesus said as we get older, things happen to us: we grow up, and we change. We have to make decisions to let go of some things like diapers, bottles, and pacifiers. **Hold up the pacifier.** He even said when we go through the biggest change of all ... when we go to heaven ... some very big changes are going to occur. We will never have to brush our teeth again. And, we will never have to take a nap, and we will never have to eat all our broccoli again. Did Jesus say that? *(no)* You're right, he didn't say it exactly in those words, but he did say when we get to heaven some very big changes are going to take place. **(Optional:** He said we won't have to get married ... I know some of you are very happy about that ... and no one will ever die again.) You will no longer have just one or two brothers and sisters; you'll have millions of brothers and sisters. We will all be one big family. We will all have one Father and we shall all be God's children. That will be the biggest change of all!

Let's Pray: Father, we look forward to growing up and the changes to come, but more than all that we look forward to the biggest change to come: being in heaven with you. Amen.

Proper 27
2 Thessalonians 2:1-5, 13-17

The First Fruit Is Always The Best

Exegetical Aim: To compare good fruit to the life we are given in Christ. Note: Some translations (the N.I.V. for example) do not include the phrase "because God chose you as his first fruits" in verse 13 and have relegated it to a footnote.

Props: Some good fruit and some bad fruit, a box or basket, and a large tray. Put the fruit on the large tray.

Lesson: Who here likes to eat? Well, I've brought some good things to eat today. Not candy, or popcorn, or pizza, but really good food. **Show the tray of fruit to the children and set it in front of them.** What I'm going to do with the fruit is put it into a basket **put the basket before you** so that I can give it to someone for the holidays. Maybe this is something that you can do at home. You might know of someone who is sick, or older, or alone, who might be cheered up by a basket of fruit. Talk to your dad or mom and see if you can do this as a family. But today I need your help. I need you to help me pick out which fruit is going to go into the basket. How should I decide what fruit to put in the basket? *(response)* Should I pick some with spots on them, or some without spots? *(response)* **Converse with children about the quality of the fruit so they can help you pick out the best.**

Application: Now we have a nice basket and it's nice because you helped me pick out the very best fruit. Let me ask you, when you picked the fruit did you pick the good fruit first, or the bad fruit first? *(response)* That's right, we always pick the best fruit first. The Bible tells us something like this concerning God. The Bible says that when we believe the truth of Jesus Christ, God looks on us as if we were the first fruits. If God looks on us as the first fruits, then how does God see us? As good or bad fruit? *(response)* Yes, as good fruit. And why does God see us as good fruit? *(response)*

218

God looks at us as if we are the best fruit because we have believed in his Son. He has picked us and included us in his basket. He has included us in his family.

Let's Pray: Thank you, Lord, for giving us the truth of Jesus Christ, and for letting us be the first fruits in your kingdom. Amen.

Proper 28
Luke 21:5-19

What Do The Signs Say?

Exegetical Aim: The relationship between world disasters and our faith. I will be relying on Jesus' interpretation in 21:11, 25-28.

Props: A bed pillow, picture of the moon, child's pajamas (or anything symbolic of the end of the day), and some photos — if you can get them — of a world disaster (Be discreet — no dead bodies of animals or people, just destroyed crops, buildings, etc.)

Lesson: We are going to play hide-and-seek this morning. Does everyone know how to play hide-and-seek? *(yeah!)* Now I have hidden three things around the front of the church. You have to find them. Here is your hint. The three things are signs that the end of the day is near. Do you understand that? You have to find the three things that tell us that the day is almost over. **Send the children out, describing the general location of the items. If your sanctuary is small, you might hide the items in the whole sanctuary to get the children among the adults. When they have returned with the items:** Our first sign is a _____. **Hold up the picture of the moon.** What is this? *(the moon)* The moon. How is the moon a sign that the end of the day is near? *(response)* Our second sign is a _____. **Hold up the pajamas.** What are these? *(pajamas)* Pajamas. How are pajamas a sign that the end of the day is coming? *(response)* Our third sign is a _____. **Hold up the bed pillow.** What is this? *(pillow)* A pillow. How is a pillow a sign that the day has ended? *(response)*

Application: These three things are signs that the day is coming to an end and it is time to go to bed. There are always signs around us telling what's about to happen. Jesus talked about signs. He said that there will be earthquakes, hunger, and terrible disasters. He said these would all be signs that God is coming to save us. (**Luke 21:11, 25-28**) How many of you have ever seen photographs of a tornado or hurricane? *(response)* Tell me what happens in a tornado or a hurricane. *(response)* A hurricane is like a really big tornado and it does a lot of damage and it hurts a lot of people. **If you have photos, discuss them at this time.** People can lose everything in these storms. They even lose pillows, pajamas, and their beds.

Jesus knew that there would be terrible events like this. And he wanted us to know that these are signs that he will be coming back. He said, "When these things begin to take place, stand up and lift up your heads, because I am about to save you." **(vs. 28, 34)** When terrible things happen, God wants us to look up in joy, hope, and trust. Remember tonight when you see the signs **hold up the pillow** that the day has ended, remember also that there are signs all around us that Jesus will soon return and save us. God wants us to have hope!

Let's Pray: Dear Lord, when we go to sleep tonight on our pillows and in our pajamas we will remember that some people are going through hard times. We know you will come one day and save us from these disasters. Amen.

Proper 28
2 Thessalonians 3:6-13

Do What Is Right

Exegetical Aim: To demonstrate that we should not be weary in doing what is right.

Props: Three stuffed animals that you will use as puppets (two alike and one a dog, e.g., two toy birds and a toy dog), a wallet, and a piece of candy.

Lesson: Introduce the two puppets as John and Joe. All through the story have them talk and walk as needed. I want to tell you a story about John and Joe. They were brothers who wanted to go for a walk. Their mother told them that if they were good, they could have a piece of candy when they returned home. So they went on their walk. After a short time, they came across a puppy dog. **Have the toy dog lying on the floor or on a table where everyone can see it.** The puppy dog was lost. John said, "I think we should help that puppy dog find its way home." Joe said, "Nah, I don't feel like it. Let's just go on." But John looked at its tag, and found that the address on the tag was just around the corner. So he took the dog home.

Then they went a little further. They found a wallet lying in the road. **Just as the stuffed animal was laid out previously, have the wallet out in the open before you begin.** John said, "We need to find out who owns the wallet and get it back to them." Joe said, "Nah, I don't feel like it. I'm getting tired. Let them find it themselves." But John picked up the wallet and found that it belonged to a man who lived just up the street. So he took the wallet to the man.

When they got home, their mother asked if they were good. What do you think? *(response)* Both boys said that they were good. So the mother asked what they did. John told the mother how they had found the dog and the wallet, and took them to their owners. Joe said, "I told him to come on, but he went ahead anyway." The mother said, "Why did you tell him to come on when he saw the dog and wanted to help it?" Joe said, "Because I just didn't feel like it." So the mother said, "Well then, only John gets a piece of candy, because only John was good." **Have John pick up a piece of candy that is sitting out.** Joe said, "But I didn't hurt anyone or anything. I wasn't bad!" The mother replied, "No, but when there is something you can do to help and you don't do it, then you have not been good and you should not be rewarded."

Application: Why didn't Joe get any candy? *(response)* That's right. Joe didn't have a good excuse for not helping the dog or for not helping with the wallet, did he? Neither do we have good excuses when we choose not to help someone who is in need. The Apostle Paul said that we should never ever get tired of doing good things. And he said that people shouldn't get rewarded if they don't want to help do good things. You see, Jesus gave everything because he loves us. Jesus was so good to us, and he never got tired of being good. We should always try to do the right thing and be like Jesus!

Let's Pray: Help us, dear Lord, never to get tired of doing good things. In Jesus' name. Amen.

Christ The King
Luke 23:33-43

How Much?

Exegetical Aim: The extent of God's love for us expressed in the actions of Christ.

Props: A large cross. Lay it down behind you out of the way.

Lesson: I want to ask you a few questions this morning. How much do you like broccoli? *(response)* No? You don't like broccoli? Not even a little bit? **Put your thumb and index finger together indicating a little bit.** Okay. I have another question. How much do you like wearing a dress? *(response)* **No doubt you'll get a mixed response along party lines. Ask one of the boys:** You don't like wearing a dress? *(response)* Not even a little bit? **Again, put your thumb and index finger together indicating a little bit.** All right, let me ask the girls. How much do you like wearing a dress? *(response)* You like wearing dresses a lot, don't you? **Spread your thumb and finger apart indicating a lot.** I have another question. How much do you like bugs? *(response)* **Perhaps this will bring another split along party lines. Ask one of the girls who winced:** You mean, you don't like crawling bugs? *(response)* She doesn't like bugs at all. Let me ask the boys. How much do you like bugs? *(response)* Some of you like them a lot? **Again, spread your fingers apart.**

I have another question. How much do you like pizza? *(response)* Now, I've found something everybody likes. You like it this much? *(response)* **Hold your hands about two feet apart.** Wow, that's a lot! You must really like pizza. Another question: How much do you like your grandma and grandpa? *(response)* **It is hoped they will begin using their hands to convey their affections.** How much? *(response)* This much? **Hold your hands about three feet apart. If one of the children says, "I love my grandma and grandpa," then say,** Oh, you *love* your grandma and grandpa? **If they don't say love then suggest it:** If you like them this much then you must *love* your grandma and grandpa. I have one more question. How much do you *love* your mom and your dad? *(response)* How much? *(response)* **They should be stretching their arms to their limit.** Boy, that's a lot of love! Let me see that again? How much do you love your mom and dad? *(response)*

Application: I have one last question. How much do you think God loves you? *(response)* How much? *(response)* You're right. **Now slowly spread your long arms straight out and say.** He loves us this much. And we know this because **bring the cross out** long ago Jesus spread his arms *way out* and some people who didn't know what they were doing put him on this cross. They put his right arm here and his left arm here and he hung there on this cross, and he said, "I love you **indicate the two points of the cross** this much." When you see the cross, remember God is quietly telling you, **having put the cross down in your lap and spreading your arms out again** how much he loves you.

Let's Pray: Oh, Lord, how much you love us. You showed how much by spreading your arms way apart. Amen.

Christ The King
Colossians 1:11-20

Mirror Image

Exegetical Aim: To know Jesus is to know God.

Props: A mirror that can be held in one hand.

Lesson: Begin by standing or sitting with your back to the children and view the children through the mirror. As the children arrive greet them by name. Good morning. You all look very nice today. **Make a comment about how a couple of the children are dressed or what they are doing.**

How am I able to see you when I am not facing you? *(response)* **Now turn around and hold out the mirror.** That's right. I can see your reflection in the mirror. Mirrors are neat things. Mirrors give us reflections of things. Where do we use mirrors? *(response)*

What's really great about mirrors is that sometimes you can use them to see things that you wouldn't ordinarily get to see. Dentists use them in our mouths so they can see in places where their eyes cannot get to. Mechanics use them sometimes to see under a car where it is difficult to reach. Mirrors give us a reflection of things so we will know what's there even if we can't see it.

Application: The Bible says this about Jesus. Here is a sentence I want you to memorize with me: Jesus is the image of the invisible God. **Have the children repeat the previous sentence a couple of times.** What that means is that we cannot see God. But if we want to know what God is like, all we have to do is look at the life of Jesus. Jesus' life is like a mirror of God. So sometimes when you wonder what God is like, just remember to look at the mirror of God. And who is the mirror of God? *(response)* That's right; Jesus is the mirror of God.

Let's Pray: Lord Jesus, when we look at you we see God. You are the image of the invisible God. Amen.

Scripture Index